DELIVERANCE

JEANETTE STRAUSS

I have purposely used the Scriptures from the Amplified Bible and the New Living Translation Bible because they are easily understood, and this book is meant to be as easy to understand as possible, whether you are new to this type of ministry or a veteran prophetic intercessor.

Please note that the name "satan" and all names related to him are not capitalized. I have made a conscious decision not to capitalize his name, even to the point of violating grammar rules.

Published by *Glorious Creations Publications*:
www.gloriouscreations.net

ISBN: 978-0-9907742-8-0

Cover by James Nesbit Prepare the Way Ministries, International
www.ptwministries.com

TABLE OF CONTENTS

Chapter 1 Is Deliverance important for a Christian?   3

Chapter 2 How can a Christian have a demon?   13

Chapter 3 Beware of lying signs and wonders   29

Chapter 4 Jesus gives us authority to operate in His name   35

Chapter 5 Long Distance deliverance   43

Chapter 6 Deliverance questions   49

Chapter 7 Ways demons can enter a person   69

Chapter 8 Practical aspects of deliverance   75

Chapter 9 The importance of identifying the Strongman   85

Chapter 10 Guide for group or self-deliverance   89

Chapter 11 Beginning the deliverance session   97

   1. Strongman of fear   101

   2. Strongman of doubt and unbelief   104

   3. Strongman of rejection   107
      a. Demon of unforgiveness   110
      b. Demon spirit of offense   111
      c. Demon spirit of anger   113
      d. Demon of an orphan spirit   114
      e. Demon spirit of resentment and bitterness   115

   4. Strongman of bondage   119

5. Strongman of heaviness/grief   121

6. Strongman of Infirmity   126

7. Strongman of a deaf and dumb spirit   128
   a. Demon spirit of suicide   131

8. Strongman of Jealousy   133

9. Strongman of Perversion   135

10. Strongman of haughtiness   140

11. Strongman of rebellion   142

12. Strongman of Antichrist   143
   a. Demon spirit of error   145
   b. Demon spirit of whoredoms   146
   c. Demon spirit of divination   147
   d. Demon of spirit of familiar spirits   148
   e. Demon spirit of sorcery   150
   f. Demon spirit of witchcraft   151
   g. Demon of a lying spirit   152

Chapter 12 Keeping Your deliverance   155

Foreword

And these signs will accompany those who believe:
In My name, they will drive out demons,
they will speak in new tongues. Mark 16:17 NIV

Jesus gave us many examples of deliverance. He performed it, taught it, and commissioned His disciples to do it. We, as believers, are disciples of Jesus. Deliverance isn't a special calling for a select few. Every believer has a responsibility to get themselves set free and then to set the captives free.

This book provides a Biblical understanding of how this part of the Kingdom of God works as it relates to deliverance. The Scriptures will stir up your faith and you will be empowered to not only set yourself free, in some cases through self-deliverance, but you will be able to help others escape their bondage.

Any believer who is not equipped to perform their role of ministry in deliverance will pay a price in their earthly life.

My people are destroyed for lack of knowledge.
Hosea 4:6 NIV

This book can easily be used for a Bible study. Your group can go over a chapter a week and go through the deliverance together as a group. The advantage of using this book is that it takes the mystery out of the subject and empowers you to get set free right away by following the step-by-step directions If you need further help, you can search out a deliverance minister.

I have personalized many of the Scriptures that will be decreed in different areas of the book.

> *I sought the Lord,*
> *and He answered me*
> *and delivered me*
> *from all my fears.*
>
> *Psalm 34:4*

Chapter 1

Is Deliverance important for a Christian?

When a Christian hears the word *deliverance*, it may evoke thoughts of fear or uncertainty. Their first thought may be, "I'm a believer in Christ, so the subject of deliverance doesn't pertain to me." According to the New Testament, this is not true.

The topic of deliverance is a foundational subject that every believer in Jesus Christ needs to understand. Deliverance of demons was important in the ministry of Jesus. He taught His disciples to perform deliverance because it was important to set the captives free so they would be successful in their walk as believers in Him.

Jesus came to earth to set people free. He said in *Luke 4:18,*

> *"The Spirit of the Lord is upon Me (the Messiah)
> Because He has anointed Me to preach the good news
> to the poor. He has sent Me to announce the release
> (pardon, forgiveness) to the captives, and recovery of
> sight to the blind, to set free those who are oppressed
> (downtrodden, bruised, crushed by tragedy).*

Following His example, we can see that being a minister of deliverance does not require a pastor's license or a college degree. The Scriptures reveal that most of the disciples were fishermen, unprofessional men.

> *Now when the men of the Sanhedrin (Jewish High
> Court) saw the confidence and boldness of Peter and John
> and grasped the fact that they were uneducated and*

3

untrained [ordinary] men, they were astounded and began to recognize that they had been with Jesus. Acts 4:13

His mission is our mission and our commission

Jesus gave His life so that we wouldn't need to suffer in the bondage that demons put us under. He taught His disciples about deliverance by educating them about the demons in the kingdom of darkness. Then He demonstrated them how to evict them, so those who believed in Him could live an enjoyable life in the Kingdom of light while still here on the earth.

If this issue about demons and deliverance is not addressed at the beginning of a person's walk with Christ, it has the power to affect their spiritual progress towards maturity. Even though, when a person accepts Jesus and they are transferred into the Kingdom of God, some of the kingdom of darkness may be hanging on within their old soulish mindsets (the old carnal man) and they are not aware of it.

That is not to say that all the difficult things that believers go through are demonic. We live on this earth and Jesus says we are not immune to trials and temptations. He will be with us, and we can live a life of victory despite our circumstances.

It is difficult to feel successful in our lives if there is a demon who is bound and determined that we won't be victorious, and he is working against us from the inside.

Some may agree that their issues could be coming from satan and that they are under attack from demons, but may believe the attack to be external, coming from the outside. It may not occur to them that it could be coming from the inside, from a demon operating within them. This subject does not fit the saying, "Ignorance is bliss," or "What you don't know won't hurt you." The topic of deliverance fits exactly with the Isaiah

5:13 Scripture that says, *Therefore my people are gone into captivity, because [they have] no knowledge.* The following story is my testimony of what happened to me shortly after I was born again. I had been saved as a child, meaning that I believed Jesus was the son of God and had died on the cross for my sins. I knew that because of my belief and confession of faith I was saved.

I did not know that I needed to cultivate a personal relationship with Jesus. I just knew I was saved, and He was in my heart because I had repented of my sins, asked for forgiveness, and asked Him to come and live in me. But that was all the further I went with any personal relationship with Jesus.

Years passed and I did not do anything to develop my relationship with Him. I believed in Jesus, occasionally went to church, listened to Bible stories, and thought that was all that was necessary.

When the following experience happened to me, I did not know about deliverance other than what I had read about in the Bible. I knew Jesus delivered people of demons, but I thought that was for them back in Bible times. They were interesting stories, but not for today, and especially not for me. I had never heard about demons in our day.

Shortly after becoming born again in my early twenty's, I found out that at least one demon was residing in me without my knowledge. That demon did not like me getting born again. Because a demon cannot get born again it began to give me problems. I could not figure out why some unusual problems were happening to me when I was so full of joy as a born-again believer. It was a shock to me when I discovered that I had that foreign body called a demon living inside of me and that it was successfully affecting my life.

5

My testimony

My husband and I had just become born-again believers. Our oldest son was under 6 months old and, as it is with a baby, he usually woke up to be fed around 2:00 am.

Early one morning, I got up to go to the kitchen to get a bottle of formula heated up. I suddenly, and without any warning, became too fearful to walk through the house. This fear did not make sense in the natural. The inside of our house was not dark at night. We lived in town on a street that was well lit with streetlights. The light coming through the windows softly illuminated every room in our home. I could clearly see where I was going as I walked through the house.

For the first time in my life I began to see in the spirit. I did not understand about seeing in the spirit at the time, but I saw rows and rows of sharp knives coming at me as I walked. Even though they did not hit me, it appeared as if they would. I could feel my heart begin to pound and every hair on my head stood up on end. I knew in my head the knives weren't real, so I talked my way through it and was successful, yet fearful, in getting my son fed that morning.

After feeding him he fell right back to sleep, and I laid him in his crib and began my walk—which turned into a run—back to our bed. I jumped into bed, pulled the covers over my head, and waited for my racing heart to return to normal. My mind was trying to figure out what had happened to me. I finally relaxed and was able to fall back to sleep.

Suddenly, I was abruptly awakened with the feeling that my arms were bound tightly at my sides. I could not move or speak. My husband was sleeping peacefully next to me, and I was helpless to do anything to wake him up to help me.

6

I was in a panic and the only thing I could think of was to shout the words "The blood of Jesus, the blood of Jesus" over and over in my mind. I could not make any physical sound come out of my mouth. Whatever was binding me suddenly released me. I sat up on the edge of the bed and I asked out loud, "Lord Jesus what is this?" I heard one word reverberate loudly through my mind. FEAR. After a long while, I was able to fall back to sleep.

In the morning I told my husband what had happened to me and what I had heard. He suggested we ask our pastor if he would know anything about this. Later that morning I called the pastor and explained what had happened. He said that he believed he knew what was going on and he would teach about it at the upcoming Friday night prayer meeting.

For the next two nights we prayed that nothing would attack me in the night, and my husband agreed to take over the 2:00 am feeding so we would not give fear a chance. It didn't bother him, and I was able to sleep without incident the next two nights.

While I was waiting for Friday night, I decided to do some research to find out if there were any places in the Bible that talked about fear. I found a Scripture that said the fear of the Lord was a good thing.

The [reverent] fear of the Lord [that is, worshiping Him and regarding Him as truly awesome] is the beginning and the preeminent part of wisdom [its starting point and its essence], And the knowledge of the Holy One is understanding and spiritual insight.
Proverbs 9:10

I also found and began to quote this Scripture before going to sleep each night.

Do not fear [anything], for I am with you; Do not be afraid, for I am your God. I will strengthen you, be assured I will help you; I will certainly take hold of you with My righteous right hand [a hand of justice, of power, of victory, of salvation]. Isaiah 41:10

I knew the type of fear I had experienced was not a good thing, and then I found a Scripture that explained it. To my surprise, the Scripture called fear a spirit. It said that the spirit of fear did not come from God.

For God did not give us a spirit of timidity or cowardice or fear, but [He has given us a spirit] of power and of love and of sound judgment and personal discipline [abilities that result in a calm, well-balanced mind and self-control]. 2 Timothy 1:7

Then I read this Scripture which made me say, "Lord Jesus, deliver me of this fear."

I sought the Lord, and He answered me and delivered me from all my fears. Psalm 34:4 ESV

When I prayed this Scripture and asked the Lord to deliver me, He did not choose to do it right at that time

The Lord instantly delivers some when they call on Him in this way. He is faithful to His Word, but His schedule is not usually the same one we are on, and He knows best. He had another plan to deliver me, which fit better with the ministry that I would become a part of in the future.

I was so happy when Friday night came. I went to the meeting with great expectation. I was hoping that the issue I had with fear would be dealt with and finished. The pastor said that he was going to share about the subject of deliverance. I listened intently to every word he was saying. What he was sharing was such a revelation to me concerning the kingdom of darkness and how it operated on earth, in our personal lives, and in our bodies.

Gradually, a strange thing began to happen. Even though I was only about six feet from him, as he was speaking his voice began to sound further and further away. The volume of his voice continued to get lower and lower. I had to lean forward in my seat and really strain to hear what he was saying. I immediately thought to myself, this is what I need for sure: deliverance.

The pastor went through the Scriptures, assuring us that deliverance was one of the assignments that Jesus gave to his disciples. They were to expel demons from people. As he taught, I wondered why I had never heard about this.

When he finished, he said that he and the leaders would be praying for people who thought they needed deliverance and wanted to be set free. He asked those who did not want prayer to leave, and those who had experienced deliverance and were familiar with this subject to stay if they wanted to assist.

There were about ten of us who felt we needed deliverance. We stood in a line and the pastor began to pray with the first person in line. I was third in the line. He and a couple of others were praying with the first person in line, when that person began to jerk around and then they began to cough and choke.

The pastor commanded the demon not to manifest or hurt the person in any way. He told the person to command the demon to come out in the name of Jesus. When that first person in line began to command the demon to go, there was an immediate reaction from the girl standing next to me line.

Suddenly she screamed out a blood-curdling scream and collapsed on the floor. I about jumped out of my skin. I did not realize it at the time, but that spirit of fear living within me was scared. It realized it was about to be evicted and was hoping to scare me into getting out of there. It didn't work.

A couple of people began to minister to the person next to me and I was all eyes and ears. I knew her to be a quiet reserved woman. They began to instruct her to command the spirit of fear to come out of her and not to manifest. As I listened to them minister to her, and as she began to command the spirit of fear to come out of her, I suddenly felt something begin to move around in my stomach and begin to move up into my throat. I began to cough.

I decided to command the spirit to get out of me too. As I did that, I felt it leave as I coughed. I heard the girl next to me coughing as the spirit left her too. The others in line were coughing and commanding the demons to leave also. That night we all got set free from various demons!

I had experienced a dramatic manifestation of God's supernatural power—and I wanted more of it! I was free of fear. I knew it was gone because I had physically felt it go. I was not afraid to get up in the night and walk through the house ever again. I became fearless, and my goal was to learn all I could about this subject and help as many others as I could.

As I thought about my experience later, I realized that what could have clued me into the fact that a demon was *inside* of me was when I repeated the words 'The blood of Jesus' over and over in my mind, it could hear me and had to respond. If it had been on the outside oppressing me, it wouldn't have been able to hear me unless I spoke out loud, which I wasn't able to do.

This is where a personal experience of deliverance comes in handy. No one would be able to convince a person that a Christian cannot harbor a demon within them, if the person they are trying to convince of that has had a personal experience of being delivered of a demon.

When I think back over the things the Lord has asked me to do since I became a Christian, I think that if I had not been exposed to the demon of fear in the way that I was, and if I had not gotten delivered of that demon of fear, I wouldn't have been able to accomplish many of the things the Lord has ordained for me to do during my time here on earth.

What Jesus taught His disciples about deliverance
After my deliverance, I was determined to learn more about the subject. I was surprised to read in the Bible that Jesus taught a lot about this subject.

The word *deliver* is mentioned 296 times in the Bible. The word *delivered* is mentioned 290 times. The word *deliverance* is mentioned sixteen times.

Deliverance: the action of being rescued or set free. In Christianity, deliverance ministry refers to the activity of cleansing a person of demons and evil spirits to address problems manifesting in their life, and the root causes of their authority to oppress the person.

Demons represent darkness and all darkness signifies the kingdom of darkness. As people are transformed into the kingdom of light through their salvation and born-again experience, if demons are within them, problems are guaranteed to occur.

As I began to fill myself with light by reading the Bible daily—the darkness manifested.

...and giving joyful thanks to the Father, who has qualified you to share in the inheritance of his holy people in the kingdom of light. For He has rescued us and has drawn us to Himself from the dominion of darkness and has transferred us to the kingdom of His beloved Son. Colossians 1:12-13 NIV

Without the spiritual knowledge that I had two opposing kingdoms living within me, I wouldn't know how to fight the battle that was going on in me. I thank the Lord that we were in a church that had a pastor who knew how to explain in a simple way what was happening and what to do about it.

Jesus repeatedly demonstrated in His ministry the existence of these two opposing kingdoms. His ministry was like a reality show every day. The disciples learned by example of the power and authority a relationship with the man Jesus and His name carried in the spiritual realm. The demons were afraid of Him even before He was crucified. They recognized who He was and the power over them that He carried.

Most of the people He ministered deliverance to were members of local synagogues. They were religious people. I am sure they were as shocked as I was when they found out they had demons operating within them.

So, He went throughout Galilee, preaching [the gospel] in their synagogues and casting out demons. Mark 1:39

Chapter 2

How can a Christian have a demon?

I have people say that a Christian can't be *possessed* by a demon, and I agree with that. But they can be *oppressed*. They usually say oppression comes from a demon who is on the outside of a person, not on the inside. When they word it that way, they are implying that they don't believe a person can have a demon residing in them.

A Christian can certainly be oppressed, from either the outside or the inside. From experience, I do know that believers can have one or more demons living within them and be oppressed by them.

A believer cannot be *possessed* because that word implies complete ownership. Jesus and the Holy Spirit within a person cannot be possessed. But demons can live within our soulish mindsets and carnal natures and compel us to continue our sinful habits.

In Greek, the word for devils is *daimonizomenous,* which means demonized. The better way to describe a person who has a demon in them is the word demonized, which is a person afflicted by a demon.

The difference between demon oppression and demon possession

Oppression is the state of being subject to unjust treatment or control, mental pressure, or distress.

In demonic oppression, the demon works to manipulate a person's behavior by the way they think. A person who is under demonic oppression may show signs of changes in their personality or attitude that are different than how they may have thought before, but they retain control over their physical body and mind.

Demons can oppress from the outside of a person as well as from the inside.

I believe we can be very influenced by demons that attack us and our minds from the outside. Just as I had the experience of being oppressed and attacked by the spirit of fear from the inside, I also had an experience of being oppressed by the spirit of fear from the outside.

I have shared the following testimony concerning the spirit of fear in another book, but it will be new to some.

Because of my background of being a member of a praise and worship dance ministry, I was asked by my pastor to teach a group of women an Israeli folk dance that he wanted us to perform for a city-wide gathering of churches for a praise, worship, and prayer session for our city. There were about fifteen dancers, and we were ready and waiting to go into the sanctuary the night of the gathering.

The church was full. We were in the foyer waiting for our time to go in when I began to hear fear manifesting among the women. None of them had ever performed a dance in front of people and they were nervous.

I heard things like, "I rebuke you fear." "I bind you fear." It was obvious if we did not go into the sanctuary soon this virus of fear would spread and maybe cause some to back out.

I decided to get everyone in a circle to pray. I think the Holy Spirit made an intervention because at that time I was in the habit of saying "I come against you fear and command you to leave" But in this instance, I found myself asking the Lord, "What shall we do about this fear?" Suddenly the Holy Spirit answered me in my mind and said, "Invite fear to come along and worship Me at the front of the church." I began to laugh at that, then I thought, "How simple and perfect!"

I said to the women, "The Lord says we should invite fear to come along with us and worship Him at the front of the church." We all dissolved in laughter! I addressed fear and said, "Fear, we are inviting you to come along and worship the Lord with us at the front of the church. But you may want to think about this because the Word of God says that when the presence of the Lord comes, He burns up all His enemies in His midst." We could almost hear the back door slam as fear ran out!

Fire goes before Him. And burns up His adversaries on all sides. Psalm 97:3

I am not saying that these women had that spirit of fear *in* them, but fear took advantage and attacked them.

Several years later I again experienced how fear could operate against us from the outside.

It happened while I was on a visit to Israel. My mother was with me, and we were staying with a friend who lived there. One warm afternoon I decided to walk down to the corner grocery store to buy some ice cream for us to have as a snack. Our friend lived in a nice quiet neighborhood, so I felt it was safe to go out alone.

I left the apartment and walked down the sidewalk toward the grocery store at the end of the block. I was about halfway to the store when suddenly I felt an evil presence surround me. I could literally feel the fear closing me in. I remembered the Scripture in Exodus where God described the darkness that would come over Egypt to Moses. It was a darkness of fear that could be felt.

> Then the Lord said to Moses, "Stretch out your hand toward heaven, that there may be darkness over the land of Egypt, a darkness to be felt."
> Exodus 10:21 ESV

I could feel the pressure of it all around me, pressing in on me. It was threatening me in the physical realm. The only way to explain it is to say that it felt like I was being attacked. It was an overwhelming feeling of a dark brooding, fearsome heaviness.

My flight or fight reflex kicked in and the adrenaline began to pump. I felt confused and found that I could hardly pray. I began to pray in tongues. Suddenly I remembered the dance experience, how fear had attacked us and how we dealt with it. I felt faith arise and replaced the fear with holy boldness.

Confidently, I said out loud, "Hello fear! I recognize you. So, you came to visit again. This is what we are going to do. We are going to sing a song together." I began to sing the song, Oh the blood of Jesus, oh the blood of Jesus, oh the blood of Jesus that washes white as snow!"

The reaction was immediate. I could sense a shaking and a quaking in the spiritual atmosphere surrounding me. By the time I said the word "blood" the second time, all fear, and anyone else who had come with him, had evaporated as quickly as they had come.

I went along my way, softly singing and rejoicing the rest of the way to the grocery store and back to the apartment, praising Jesus.

The song that says, *There is power in the Blood,* is true. It was an amazing experience. There was no battle on my part to try to overcome those warfare spirits that were attacking, me. My praise and the Blood of Jesus won the victory! I have never dealt with that spirit of fear since that time, not from the inside or from the outside. If it ever attacks me again, I am equipped with the knowledge and understanding of how to get rid of it. I hope that what I've shared helps you too.

Possession

Possession is the state of having, owning, or controlling something. an item of property; something belonging to one.

With demonic possession, a demon called a 'strongman' will have complete control of a person's mind and body. This can easily come from drug addiction or other various reasons. The demon takes control and removes the person's ability to use his physical body, will, consciousness, and freedom. The person usually adopts the personality, voice, and actions of an alternate personality or a demon. By using the person's body, it communicates to other people by using a different voice and actions.

Evil spirits are constantly looking for ways to get into a person's body. We have discussed how people open doors into their lives not realizing the repercussions.

Jesus rebuked an evil spirit within the disciple Peter.

> But Jesus turned and said to Peter, "Get behind Me, Satan! You are a stumbling block to Me; for you are not setting your mind on things of God, but on things of man." Matthew 16:23

This spirit was trying to use Peter's mind, will, and emotions to influence Jesus to get off track.

A person may be told that they were delivered when they get saved because only worldly people have demons. We agree that our sin goes under the blood of Jesus when we get saved, and our spirit has been endued and empowered with the Holy Spirit of God and has had a transformation.

The demons that may be inside of us live in the regions of our soul man which includes our mind, will, and emotions, but not our spirit, because that is where the Holy Spirit lives. They live in a different neighborhood within us.

We cannot put the demon or demons who might be residing in us under the blood of Jesus until we have renewed our minds. If we don't have renewed minds, there will be an internal battle.

The Amplified Bible speaks of the inner man that must have a life change. The inner man is the soulish carnal nature of man.

> "The [appointed period of] time is fulfilled, and the kingdom of God is at hand; repent [change your inner self—your old way of thinking, regret past sins, live your life in a way that proves repentance; seek God's purpose for your life] and believe [with a deep, abiding trust] in the good news [regarding salvation]."
> Mark 1:15

As disciples of Christ, we have been given the same mission that was given to Jesus. It is found in Luke 4:18:

> The Spirit of the Lord is upon me because he has anointed me to proclaim good news to the poor. He has sent me to proclaim liberty to the captives and

*recovering of sight to the blind, to set at liberty those
who are oppressed. (NIV)*

Some new believers run into resistance in areas they have
struggled with in the past. They cannot figure out why they
struggle with old problems that they expected to be free of. It
can be confusing because the Word says that all things
become new when they accept Christ and old things are
washed away.

Most of us are aware of the Scripture,

> *Therefore, if anyone is in Christ, the new creation has
> come: The old has gone, the new is here!
> 2 Corinthians 5:17 NIV*

There are challenges to overcome as we are becoming a new
creation. As we are re-created over the course of our lives,
God gradually helps us to replace the old "program" we were
living in day by day with a new one – His.

As we read His Word and begin to cultivate a new culture in
our lives, we begin to love and be attracted to the new style
of living that the Holy Spirit is developing within each of us.
We begin at both a subconscious and conscious level to reject
the things that Jesus rejects, embracing the teachings in the
Bible. We begin to display the fruits of living a spirit-filled life.

> *The fruit of the Spirit is love, joy, peace, patience,
> kindness, goodness, faithfulness, gentleness, self-
> control. Galatians 5:22–23a ESV*

As we change it does not go unnoticed by others, and there
will be opportunities to lead others to Christ just by them
seeing the change in us.

When Bud and I began to go to church and really got born
again and baptized in the Holy Spirit, we must have changed

so much that our family members began to ask us questions. I remember a family member asking me a specific question after we had been going to church for about two months. We had just enjoyed a family get-together meal with some relatives. As we were doing dishes one of them asked me; "What is going on with you guys?" I asked, "What do you mean?" She said, "You seem so happy. You and Bud seem changed in a way that I can't put my finger on."

I knew that she had heard from other relatives that we had started going to church but we had not yet invited them to go. So, I said, "I guess it is because we have started going to church every week and are reading the Bible. It's changing us and our marriage, and we love our new way of life."

Then I asked her if they would like to go to church with us. They had gone to church years ago and accepted Jesus but did not go to church anywhere. She said they wanted to go, and it was not long until quite a few members of our family began going to church and developed a relationship with Christ. They were all filled with the Holy Spirit, baptized, and began going to church every week and living changed lives.

After this experience, I began to realize how people watch us. We can have an effect on those we are close to as we begin to manifest the fruit of the spirit in our lives towards them and others.

How can a demon live inside of us?
After we are born again, our newborn spirit is hungry for the things of God. Everything seems new. Believers will testify to this change and the joy it brings. We become new in the spirit area of our bodies; the spirit of man belongs to God, and we now have the Holy Spirit living within our spirit man.

But it is a spirit in man, And the breath of the Almighty gives them understanding. Job 32:8 NIV

The Spirit of God has made me, and the breath of the Almighty gives me life. Job 33:4 NIV

We are composed of spirit, soul, and body. All goes well with our spirit after we are born again, but our soul nature may be having issues.

That which is born of the flesh is flesh, and that which is born of the Spirit is spirit. Marvel not that I said unto thee, Ye must be born again. John 3:6-7 KJV

When the Bible talks about the flesh nature of man it is referring to the physical carnal nature of man, his soul. The soul is composed of our mind, will, and emotions. When we get saved, our soul or carnal nature begins a constant spiritual transformation as we grow in the Lord.

The soul is also referred to as the heart of man and according to the Bible is 'most wicked'. The flesh or the physical body, mind, will, and emotions are influenced by satan, the world, and by its own habits built over a lifetime. It is also called a man's 'worldly nature' which is selfish and always is thinking about its own wants and desires.

The heart is deceitful above all things, and desperately wicked: who can know it? Jeremiah 17:9 KJV

This carnal part of man fights the new spiritual man that has been newly created. It was friends with the old carnal self, but the new self is aligned with God's Spirit, and the flesh can no longer be in control. This creates conflict within a person. Paul had a problem with his soul nature even though his spirit was totally new and committed to the Lord.

For I do not understand my own actions [I am baffled, bewildered]. I do not practice or accomplish what I

21

wish, but I do the very thing that I loathe [[a]which my moral instinct condemns]. Now if I do [habitually] what is contrary to my desire, [that means that] I acknowledge and agree that the Law is good (morally excellent) and that I take sides with it. However, it is no longer I who do the deed, but the sin [principle] which is at home in me and has possession of me. For I know that nothing good dwells within me, that is, in my flesh. I can know what is right, but I cannot perform it. [I have the intention and urge to do what is right, but no power to carry it out.]   Romans 7:15-20

If we are alert and know how demons operate, we will recognize their influence on us. The farther along in our Christian maturity we get, the more a demon will begin to manifest and show itself in negative patterns in our life. Others might see something is wrong and a person might sense it too, but they may not understand the real problem. If they do recognize a demon at work in their life, they probably don't know what to do about it.

The key to spiritual growth is what we choose to feed ourselves. If we feed ourselves the Word, our Spirit man will grow. If we fall back into the worldly way of thinking after getting saved, our carnal soul nature will grow, and we will grow away from our Godly spiritual way of life. We decide which one we want to grow, the spiritual man, or the carnal man.

As we read the Bible and learn from pastors and godly teachers as they discuss and study the Scriptures, the Bible relates it to seed being sown into us.

The seed falling on rocky ground refers to someone who hears the word and at once receives it with joy. But since they have no root, they last only a short time. When trouble or persecution comes because of the word, they quickly fall away. The seed falling among the thorns refers to someone who hears the word, but the worries of this life and the deceitfulness of wealth choke the word, making it unfruitful. Matthew 13:20-22 NIV

When we feed our spirit man consistently with the seed of the Word, we starve the worldly soul nature. Our soul nature begins to change. As this happens, if there is a demon or demons present in our soul area they will begin to protest. The demons do not want to listen to worship music, they don't want to go to church, and they don't want you to read the Word. They especially don't want to listen to talk about the blood of Jesus; it makes them extremely nervous. So much so that they tremble.

> *You believe that there is one God. You do well. Even the demons believe—and tremble! James 2:19 NKJV*

It is clear if a person doesn't have knowledge about the subject of demons, they may begin to listen to them speak and influence their actions. The demon's job is to plant doubt in a person. Remember, satan planted doubt in Eve's mind and he enticed her to sin and convinced her to get her husband to sin.

> *Now the serpent was more crafty (subtle, skilled in deceit) than any living creature of the field which the Lord God had made. And the serpent (Satan) said to the woman, "Can it really be that God has said, 'You shall not eat from any tree of the garden? Genesis 3:1*

Don't ever doubt the power of doubt in your life and its consequences. Sarah doubted that God was able to fulfill His Word that she would have a child in her old age and convinced Abraham to doubt also. (Genesis 16-18). The consequences of her doubt and unbelief have affected generations for centuries and still are. Our bad decisions, have

23

the potential to negatively affect our spiritual growth and those who are born after us.

The battle over our spiritual life

Ask yourself, are you enjoying the blessings of God? Or are you enduring the oppressive influence of the enemy? Do you wonder why you are not being blessed as a Christian in the same way that other Christians seem to be?

Some people seem driven to act in certain ways and believe certain things despite the fact it may be detrimental to their well-being. The question is, who is driving them and why? We all know Christians who never seem to get a break. There is something evil behind that.

God says He has come to give us life and give it more abundantly. If we are not living an abundant life, we need to examine what is really going on. Is it our own behavior and bad habits that have been working against us, or the influence of a curse with a demon attached who wants to destroy us and our faith?

And this is the judgment: the light has come into the world, and people loved the darkness rather than the light because their works were evil. For everyone who does wicked things hates the light and does not come to the light, lest his works should be exposed.
John 3:19-20 ESV

Two kingdoms

A person may desperately need deliverance but have never heard of deliverance and how it fits into the two kingdoms we deal with as believers. There is the visible physical realm we live and function in every day, and the mysterious invisible spiritual kingdom we live in at the same time.

As Kingdom of God people, we have been redeemed from the darkness of sin and death. The kingdom we became citizens of as believers is called the Kingdom of Light. There is a kingdom of darkness that we have been delivered out of which opposes the Kingdom of Light.

> For at one time, you were darkness, but now you are light in the Lord. Walk as children of light.
> Ephesians 5:8 ESV

When we accept Jesus we are new to this Kingdom of Light, like babies that have just been delivered from their mother's womb. We must grow into our new lives and our new futures. We must develop new eyesight; we must learn to see with spiritual eyes. This comes from reading the Bible and spending time with and listening to mature believers who can help us along.

> So we look not at the things which are seen, but at the things which are unseen; for the things which are visible are temporal (brief and fleeting) but the things which are invisible are everlasting and imperishable.
> 2 Corinthians 4:18

> I have given them your word and the world has hated them, for they are not of the world any more than I am of the world. My prayer is not that you take them out of the world but that you protect them from the evil one.
> John 17:14-15 NLJV

Or in other words, as believers we are *in* the world not *of* it.

Should we take it for granted that every new believer needs deliverance?

The answer to this question is "no." But each person needs to be equipped with the understanding and knowledge, not only for themselves (in case they need deliverance) but to be able to help others that might need it to enjoy a successful Christian life.

Over the past 50 years of ministry, Bud and I have seen people live their lives as believers, attending church, and working in different ministries. But in their personal lives they exist day by day, feeling defeated because of unseen barriers in areas that they can't seem to get a victory over. Most people blame themselves and think something is wrong with them.

They may have demons within who whisper to their minds, "Something bad is going to happen to you soon." They fear for their finances, health, relationships, or any number of issues in their life. Even if there does not seem to be anything to worry about, they will find something that will cause anxiety. They live with a feeling of foreboding.

This is why the Scripture tells us to test the spirits. If a person is hearing this negative input all the time from within it may be a spirit.

Beloved, do not put faith in every spirit, but prove (test) the spirits to discover whether they proceed from God; for many false prophets have gone forth into the world. By this you may know (perceive and recognize) the Spirit of God: every spirit which acknowledges and confesses [the fact] that Jesus Christ (the Messiah) [actually] has become man and has come in the flesh is of God [has God for its source]; And every spirit which does not acknowledge and confess that Jesus Christ has come in the flesh [but would [a]annul, destroy, [b]sever, disunite Him] is not of God [does not proceed from Him]. This [c] non-confession] is the [spirit] of the antichrist, [of] which you heard that it was coming, and now it is already in the world. Little children, you are of God [you belong to Him] and have [already] defeated and overcome them [the agents of the antichrist], because He Who lives in you is greater (mightier) than he who is in the world. 1 John 4:1-5

After reading this book, some may think they could benefit from deliverance. But then the enemy whispers to them, "What will people think of me if I ask for deliverance?"

If a believer thinks they may need deliverance, it does not reflect on them personally. It does not mean they are unspiritual, or sinful, or lack faith. This is a natural part of maturing in your faith.

Dear friends, do not believe every spirit, but test the spirits to see whether they are from God, because many false prophets have gone out into the world.

1 John 4:1 NIV

Chapter 3

Beware of lying signs and wonders

The Bible warns us of lying signs and wonders.

> The coming of the [Antichrist, the lawless] one is
> through the activity of Satan, [attended] with great
> power [all kinds of counterfeit miracles] and [deceptive]
> signs and false wonders [all of them lies.
> 2 Thessalonians 2:9

These lying signs and wonders do not just appear in the end days. They have been active throughout history and are still on the scene. Magicians are a good example. Look how they can fool people. They make a living by performing lying signs and wonders. I am not saying that all magicians are demonic, but I am just using them as an example of how easily people can be fooled – even when we know that what they are doing is a rehearsed act.

We read of these lying signs and wonders in the book of Exodus. God spoke to Moses through a burning bush and charged him to speak to Pharaoh on His behalf (Exodus 3). During that commissioning, God granted Moses the ability to perform miracles (Exodus 4:21).

We find in the story that Pharaoh's magicians were able to perform some of the miracles, but not all of them. The story of Pharaoh's magicians can be found in Exodus 7–8. When Moses and Aaron confront the Pharaoh in Egypt, demanding that he free the Israelites so they could go three days journey into the wilderness to worship their God. Pharaoh refused the request as God had told Moses he would. Moses and Aaron performed three miracles, to begin with, to confirm to Pharaoh that their message was from God. On those three occasions, Pharaoh's magicians were able to duplicate the miracles.

God instructed Moses and Aaron to throw down Aaron's staff upon their first meeting with the ruler. Aaron did so, and his staff turned into a snake. Pharaoh immediately summoned his magicians, who were able to turn their own staffs into snakes. In what must have been an ominous sign for Pharaoh's court, Aaron's snake then devoured the magicians' snakes (see Exodus 7:8–13).

Twice more, Pharaoh's magicians were able to perform miracles to match the signs of Moses and Aaron. The first plague that Moses called down upon the Egyptians was a plague of blood. The magicians were also able to turn water to blood as Moses had done to the Nile River (Exodus 7:14–22). The second plague was a horde of frogs sent among the Egyptian people, and the magicians summoned their own frogs as well—adding to the problem rather than alleviating it (Exodus 8:1–7). After this, however, the magicians' power stopped, as they were unable to replicate any further plagues, and they acknowledged they were witnessing "the finger of God" in Moses' signs (verse 19).

But how were the magicians of Egypt able to perform the miracles in the first place? Those magicians may have received their power from satan. Although not as powerful as God, satan, formerly one of God's highest angels, has the power to deceive, emulate miracles, and even tell the future with a certain degree of accuracy because he knows what the Bible says about the future. Satan may have given Pharaoh's magicians the power to duplicate some of the signs God performed through Moses and Aaron.

Whether they were creating illusions or performing actual miracles, the Egyptian magicians were eventually stymied by God's power. They were unable to summon gnats (Exodus 8:16–19), turn the sky dark (Exodus 10:21–23), call down hailstones (Exodus 9:22–26), or duplicate any of the other plagues. God's power is great enough to defeat both man's conniving and satan's power with ease.

We should always question where the power source is coming from when we witness signs and wonders in different settings. In the end times, false apostles and prophets will arise.

The Bible gives us a clear warning

For such men are false apostles, deceitful workmen, disguising themselves as apostles of Christ. And no wonder, for even satan disguises himself as an angel of light. So, it is no surprise if his servants, also, disguise themselves as servants of righteousness. Their end will correspond to their deeds. 2 Corinthians 11:13-15 ESV

Jesus had people following Him wherever He went, because they believed the power that He was using to deliver people of demons and heal the sick came from the God they believed in. They had heard about Him healing the man in the synagogue who had a withered arm. Quite a few trusted that He was from God because He performed that miracle in the religious setting.

Then a demon-possessed man who was blind and mute was brought to Jesus, and He healed him, so that the mute man both spoke and saw. All the people wondered in amazement, and said, "Could this be the Son of David (the Messiah)?" Matthew 12:22

The words "Son of David" give us the clue that they were religious Jews who were waiting for their Messiah to come. They wondered if this man called Jesus was from the legal lineage of King David. They could not believe this simple man could possibly have the authority given to Him by God to deliver someone of demons. That's why they accused Him of delivering demons through the power of Beelzebub.

> *Jesus was driving out a demon that was mute. When the demon left, the man who had been mute spoke, and the crowd was amazed. But some of them said, "By Beelzebul, the prince of demons, he is driving out demons." Luke 11:14-15 NIV*

Jesus didn't fit their presumed ideas of how their long-awaited Messiah would come. They were expecting Him to come as a king, and He did not fit their idea of a king. Many Old Testament Scriptures reinforce the fact that the Messiah will have to come from the lineage of David. He did have the required bloodline lineage that would be required of the Messiah, through both his mother and as the adopted son of Joseph, but they wouldn't accept Him.

> *The angel Gabriel said to Mary, the mother of Jesus, He will be very great and will be called the Son of the Most High. The Lord God will give him the throne of his ancestor David. Luke 1:32 NLT*

> *...which was spoken by Samuel to King David: "When your days are fulfilled and you lie down with your fathers, I will raise up your offspring after you, who shall come from your body, and I will establish his kingdom. He shall build a house for my name, and I will establish the throne of his kingdom forever." 2 Samuel 7:12-13 ESV*

> *Others said, "This is the Christ." But some said, "Will the Christ come out of Galilee? Has not the Scripture said that the Christ comes from the seed of David and from the town of Bethlehem, where David was?" John 7:41-42 NKJV*

Jesus knew their thoughts about Him and confronted them.

> *Now when the Pharisees heard it, they said, "This fellow does not cast out demons except by Beelzebub, the ruler of the demons." But Jesus knew their thoughts and said to them: "Every kingdom divided against itself is brought to desolation, and every city or house divided against itself will not stand. If Satan casts out Satan, he is divided against himself. How then will his kingdom stand? And if I cast out demons by Beelzebub, by whom do your sons cast them out? Therefore, they shall be your judges. But if I cast out demons by the Spirit of God, surely the kingdom of God has come upon you.* Matthew 12:24-27 NKJV

This Scripture lists two names besides Jesus in whose name demons can be cast out: satan and beelzebub. Beelzebub is a name derived from a Philistine god and is associated with the Canaanite god Baal.

In theological sources, predominantly Christian, beelzebub is sometimes another name for the devil, like satan.

Jesus is saying that if satan casts out a demon then it is like he is kicking his own family out of the house, and if he does that the house (or his family) will fall. We can be assured that satan would never want to cast a demon out of a person unless he was trying to fool and beguile people. Jesus never said that satan could not do it, but he clearly said that if he did then it would divide his kingdom.

As believers, we will have to be alert because the Word says the antichrist will perform lying signs and wonders. Deliverance always has been a sign and a wonder, so it is likely satan will use this to trick people.

Dear friends, do not believe every spirit, but test the spirits to see whether they are from God, because many false prophets have gone out into the world.
1 John 4:1 NIV

For false Christs and false prophets will appear and perform great signs and wonders that would deceive even the elect if that were possible. Matthew 24:24

This Scripture clearly says the elect will not be deceived. I have heard so many people misquote this. They say even the elect will be deceived in the end days, but that is not what it says. It does say it will be confusing. Like the media is today. Unfortunately, we cannot believe what we hear or see any more on the news coming from most of the media.

The coming of the [Antichrist, the lawless] one is through the activity of Satan, [attended] with great power [all kinds of counterfeit miracles] and [deceptive] signs and false wonders [all of them lies].
2 Thessalonians 2:9

Satan is the commander of his kingdom even though he has limited power. He most likely sent the demon to torment the person to begin with. So if a witch or ambassador of the kingdom of darkness tries to evict a demon they would be working against their leader and his kingdom would not last long, and neither would they. It is God who is the ultimate authority, and He has the final word.

Every knee will eventually bow to Him.

That at the name of Jesus every knee should bow, of things in heaven, and things in earth, and things under the earth; And that every tongue should confess that Jesus Christ is Lord, to the glory of God the Father.
Philippians 2:10–11 KJV.

Chapter 4

Jesus gives us authority to operate in His name

And Jesus came up and spoke to them, saying, "All authority has been given to Me in heaven and on earth. "Go therefore and make disciples of all the nations, baptizing them in the name of the Father and the Son and the Holy Spirit, teaching them to observe all that I commanded you; and lo, I am with you always, even to the end of the age." Matthew 28:18-20 NKJV

"Then He called His twelve disciples together and gave them power and authority over all demons, and to cure diseases. He sent them to preach the kingdom of God and to heal the sick." Luke 9:1-2 NKJV

Jesus called his twelve disciples to him and gave them authority to drive out impure spirits and to heal every disease and sickness. Matthew 10:1 NIV

He has authorized us to use his name on our behalf here on the earth. We are to go forth, commissioned by Him as His disciples, to perform His will. We carry with us the authority He has given us over the enemy.

Jesus is our example

In the synagogue there was a man possessed by a demon, an impure spirit. He cried out at the top of his voice, "Go away! What do you want with us, Jesus of Nazareth? Have you come to destroy us? I know who you are—the Holy One of God!" "Be quiet!" Jesus said sternly. "Come out of him!" Then the demon threw the man down before them all and came out without injuring him. Luke 4:33-35 NIV

Demons are not afraid of believers who do not believe that they can harbor a demon. Their greatest fear is that the person will find out about them and kick them out. They know that believers have the authority to evict them from a person. A person must agree to want deliverance, or the demon will take advantage of their reluctance and know it will not have to leave.

It may sound strange, but some people are afraid to get rid of a demon because they have wrapped their identity up in that demon. In some cases, it has talked to them their whole life and they are familiar with it. That is a *familiar spirit.* If you know someone like that, it is not our job to judge them. But it is our job to pray that the Holy Spirit will remove the veil from their eyes, and they will see the truth of how that demon is misdirecting them and keeping them from doing what God wants them to do. Pray that God will grant them the faith in Jesus to evict any demons so they can experience who they are in Christ and be set free.

Every disciple of Christ has been commissioned to perform deliverance. As believer's, the ministry of the deliverance of demons is part of our Kingdom of God assignment here on the earth–to set people free.

And these signs will accompany those who believe: In my name they will drive out demons; they will speak in new tongues. Mark 16:17 NIV

They drove out many demons and anointed many sick people with oil and healed them. Mark 6:13 NIV

This Scripture links the gift of speaking in tongues and being healed with deliverance. If you, or a person you know, have not been able to receive your tongues, a demon may be blocking your healing. Deliverance may solve that problem.

If a person cannot forgive another person, it can totally block them from receiving their prayer language of unknown tongues. Once they forgive the person or people, they can receive. I have seen this happen many times.

> *Whenever you stand praying, if you have anything against anyone, forgive him so that your Father who is in heaven will also forgive you your transgressions and wrongdoings. But if you do not forgive, neither will your Father in heaven forgive your transgressions.*
> *Mark 11:25-26*

Demons are fearful of the power that believers have over them.

Demons reside in the soul realm within us. Because they are spirits, a lot of them can fit into a small area. Remember the man who had a legion of demons in him. A Roman legion was a large military unit of the Roman army of 5,000 men.

My friends and I had an encounter with a man who I believe had multitudes of demons in him. They had succeeded in taking him captive. The Lord gave us an opportunity to minister to him in a very unconventional way, but we believe it produced great results.

Two of my friends and I were at a conference. We had tables set up in the marketplace. One night after everyone had gone back into the sanctuary after a break, we stayed back to straighten up the items on our tables before going into the session.

I was at one of the tables and my two friends were at another table when I looked up and saw a man walking around looking at the items on the other tables. He looked up and saw me watching him and he walked over to me. He was about 6 feet tall and had long blonde hair. He was dressed in a t-shirt and tan cargo-type shorts. He had sandals on his feet. He reminded me of a beach boy, except he was maybe in his 40's. With a smile on his face, he extended his hand out for me to shake so I extended my hand to him. As I was taking his hand, I saw that he had several beaded necklaces around his neck, the biggest one having about 6 little buddha's hanging from it all along the front. He said to me; "Hello. My name is Jesus Christ."

I must admit I was a little taken aback because I had never had anyone tell me they were Jesus before. I managed to keep myself together and I smiled and said, "Hello my name is Jeanette, and I am so glad you stopped to visit."

Instantly that Scripture popped into my mind that says,

> For many shall come in my name, saying, I am Christ; and shall deceive many. Matthew 24:5 KJV

I asked him, "I am curious how you know you are Jesus Christ?" He replied," Because I have been all over the world and have studied under the greatest masters." He continued, "You can ask me anything and I can give you the answer." I said, "Well, I do have something to say, but, first let's invite my friends over to meet you."

I called my friends over and he extended his hand to each of them, and they shook his hand. I said, "This is Joyce, and this is Lynn. He smiled at them and said, "My name is Jesus Christ." Their looks were priceless, like who???!!

I said to him, "We are so glad to meet you in person, because there is something we would love to do with you. He said, "Ok. What is it? Ask me anything." I said, "Well, let's walk over here by the wall away from these tables where we have more room." We walked over to the wall. He stood with his back to the wall. "We want to pray with you, but first let's hold hands." We were in a small circle; he extended his hands, and we held hands.

With a big smile on his face he waited for me to ask him a question. I said, "Before we ask you questions, we want to thank God for sending Jesus to be crucified, to become a living sacrifice for our sins." As soon as I said that he said, "NO! Don't say that." I said, "Ok, then we want to thank Jesus so much for his blood that was shed on the cross." He said loudly "Don't say that!" I replied, "OK. Then let's sing a song together." He said, "OK, what song?" I said, "One you should like." I began to sing, "Oh the blood of Jesus, oh the blood of Jesus," and the girls chimed in.

His response was immediate. He began to literally try to climb backwards up that wall while trying to get his hands loose from us. His eyes were wild with fear. I said, "You are not Jesus Christ. Jesus is the Supreme Master over everything within you. Turn away from all those foreign gods that are talking to you and give your life to Jesus Christ. He is master over them. He is able and wants to set you free from them! Call out to Him and He will hear you and deliver you. He loves you."

At that, he managed to get his hands loose and ran as fast as he could out of the place. We looked at each other and decreed: Thank You, Lord, that this was a divine appointment, and you are going to set that man free!,

We went to find the manager in charge of the marketplace and told him that there was a man who had been walking around after everyone had gone into the meeting and had introduced himself to us as Jesus Christ. We told him that we were concerned that he might scare some people.

He said he knew who the man was and that he had blown his mind on drugs. His mother attended their church and lived on the grounds, and he lived with her. The church had been praying for this young man for several years.

We shared with him what had happened, and that God was surely at work. Several years later we went back there for another conference. When I inquired about what had become of the young man, I was told that the Lord had delivered him and that he was born again and attending church. We did not see him on that trip and have not been back there, but the Lord is good, and I believe that was an example of this Scripture.

> *Preach the word [as an official messenger]; be ready when the time is right and even when it is not [keep your sense of urgency, whether the opportunity seems favorable or unfavorable, whether convenient or inconvenient, whether welcome or unwelcome]; correct [those who err in doctrine or behavior], warn [those who sin], exhort and encourage [those who are growing toward spiritual maturity], with inexhaustible patience and [faithful] teaching. 2 Timothy 4:2*

I think that the opportunity that God gave us was the exact time when the young man needed to hear what he did. It combined with the prayers of his mother, and others, ascending to heaven on his behalf.

Learn to be bold in the Holy Spirit

> *The wicked flee when no one pursues, but the righteous are bold as a lion. Proverbs 28:1*

I am thankful that the deliverances that both Bud and I have witnessed have emboldened us to utilize the power we have been given in the name of Jesus and the Blood of Jesus. The same will happen to you.

40

According to the Bible, the disciples marveled about that power and authority too. When they told Jesus those demons had to bow to His name, He acknowledged it but told them that they should be glad that they belonged to Him more than the fact they had been given the authority to deliver demons.

> However, do not rejoice that the spirits submit to you, but rejoice that your names are written in heaven." Luke 10:20 NIV

So even though we rejoice in every captive being set free, we rejoice more in our salvation.

> The seventy returned with joy, saying, "Lord, even the demons are subject to us in Your name." He said to them, "I watched Satan fall from heaven like [a flash of] lightning. Listen carefully: I have given you authority [that you now possess] to tread on serpents and scorpions, and [the ability to exercise authority] over all the power of the enemy (Satan); and nothing will [in any way] harm you. Luke 10: 17-19

Some may be hearing a voice telling them that that they are not good enough to perform deliverance. Don't let the voice convince you to disqualify yourself from this ministry. In fact, be encouraged. What is attached to that voice is very afraid of who you are in Christ.

The disciples were not perfect, but human like us. One thing that could disqualify us from the service of the Lord is pride. We are forgiven and our goal is to be more like Jesus every day. It is important to nurture a spirit of humility, especially in deliverance. The demons do not respect the authority you have within yourself as a human being, but they do respect and know they must obey the authority you carry in Jesus.

> Submit yourselves, therefore, to God. Resist the devil, and he will flee from you. James 4:7 ESV

The demons know who Jesus is and must submit to Him. Here are a few Scriptures for the purpose of building faith where deliverance is concerned.

When He arrived at the other side in the country of the Gadarenes, two demon-possessed men coming out of the tombs met Him. They were *so extremely fierce* and *violent that no one could pass by that way. And they screamed out, "What business do we have [in common] with each other, Son of God? Have You come to torment us before the appointed time [of judgment]?" Matthew 8:28-29*

When he saw Jesus from afar, he ran and worshiped Him. And he cried out with a loud voice and said, "What have I to do with You, Jesus, Son of the Most High God? I implore You by God that You do not torment me." Mark 5:6-7 NKJV

They went to Capernaum, and when the Sabbath came, Jesus went into the synagogue and began to teach. The people were amazed at his teaching because he taught them as one who had authority, not as the teachers of the law. Just then a man in their synagogue who was possessed by an impure spirit cried out, "What do you want with us, Jesus of Nazareth? Have you come to destroy us? I know who you are—the Holy One of God!"

"Be quiet!" said Jesus sternly. "Come out of him!" The impure spirit shook the man violently and came out of him with a shriek. The people were all so amazed that they asked each other, "What is this? A new teaching— and with authority! He even gives orders to impure spirits, and they obey him." Mark 1:21-27 NIV

Chapter 5

Long Distance deliverance

Jesus is not limited by time, or distance—neither are we.

After He had finished all that He had to say in the hearing of the people, He went to Capernaum. Now a [Roman] centurion's slave, who was highly regarded by him, was sick and on the verge of death. When the centurion heard about Jesus, he sent some Jewish elders to Him, asking Him to come and save the life of his slave. When they reached Jesus, they pleaded with Him earnestly [to come], saying, "He is worthy for You to do this for him, because he loves our nation, and he built us our synagogue [at his own expense]." And Jesus went with them.

But when He was near the house, the centurion sent friends to Him, saying, "Lord, do not trouble Yourself further, for I am not worthy for You to come under my roof. Therefore, I did not even consider myself worthy to come to You. But just speak a word, and my slave will be healed. For I also am a man subject to authority, with soldiers under me; and I say to this one, 'Go,' and he goes, and to another, 'Come,' and he comes, and to my slave, 'Do this,' and he does it." Now when Jesus heard this, He was amazed at him, and turned and said to the crowd that was following Him, "I say to you, not even in Israel have I found such great faith [as this man's]." When the messengers who had been sent returned to the house, they found the slave in good health. Luke 7:1-10

43

As an intercessor, I and many other believers have experienced this type of long-distance deliverance with a person. It's not unusual to pray for people to receive a deliverance over the phone, who are states, and even countries away, and they were delivered. I clearly remember one time when I prayed over the phone for a person to be delivered of a spirit of fear and trauma, and something remarkable happened.

A woman called me at my home in Michigan and identified herself as a friend of someone I knew in Florida. She said that her friend had been praying for her and suggested that she call me and ask me to pray with her.

She told me that two years earlier she had been in a restaurant with friends having dinner. She went into the restroom before leaving. There were two stalls in the bathroom. The larger stall had a sign on the door saying out of order. She went into the one next to it. She sat down and a movement behind her caught her eye when she looked down and to the back of the stall. There was a man's head sticking out of the stall next to her looking up at her. He had gone into the stall and laid down on the floor on his back and when she sat down, he had slid out from the back of the stall so his head was at the back of the toilet in her stall, and he could watch her. She said that she immediately went into a panic and began to scream. She jumped up and pulled herself together and ran out of the bathroom. She ran and asked to speak to the manager. She told him what happened, and he went into the bathroom. There was a backpack lying in the stall, but the man was gone. There was nothing in the backpack to identify him.

The fallout from this had been devastating to her. She was so full of fear that she began to have panic attacks. Her fears had grown over the last two years, and she had gotten so she could hardly leave her home. She had to give up her job. She was begging me to do something to help her. She could not go into any public restroom and hadn't been back to any restaurant.

I explained to her that a spirit of fear and trauma may have entered her when she was so frightened, and they were trying to control her. She agreed. I asked her if she was ready to get rid of them and she said yes. I told her the demons would have to go because Jesus would drive them out and the distance didn't mean anything., She could get deliverance long distance, as if I were the same room with her. She said she believed me, so she repeated after me as I led her in a prayer that went something like this:

Dear Heavenly Father, I repent on behalf of any sin that I may have committed against You in any way, and I ask forgiveness. I ask that You wash me clean with the blood of Jesus. I now command a spirit of fear and trauma, and any others that came with them that evening in the restaurant and any time before or since, to leave me now in the name of Jesus.

Suddenly there was ear piercing screams on the other end of the phone. After about three of them I said, "Stop now in the name of Jesus and get out of my sister now! You must go! No more manifesting, in the name of Jesus!"

There was silence on the other end of the line. Then I could hear soft weeping. I asked her if she was OK, and if the demons were gone. She was crying and said, "Yes they are gone! I feel wonderful. I felt them go when I screamed." They had come in on a scream and they left with one.

She was fine from then on. She called me a few months after our prayer to tell me how wonderful she felt and how Jesus completely delivered her. She could even go into a restroom in a restaurant again. She had been studying about deliverance and has a testimony to share with people when she prays for them to be delivered.

> And we know [with great confidence] that God [who is deeply concerned about us] causes all things to work together [as a plan] for good for those who love God, to those who are called according to His plan and purpose. Romans 8:28

It has always and forever will be about Jesus and the power and authority in His name.

Here is another example of Jesus performing a long-distance healing.

> So, Jesus came again to Cana of Galilee, where He had turned the water into wine. And there was a certain royal official whose son was sick in Capernaum. Having heard that Jesus had come back from Judea to Galilee, he went to meet Him and began asking Him to come down and heal his son; for he was at the point of death. Then Jesus said to him, "Unless you see [miraculous] signs and wonders, you [simply] will not believe." The royal official pleaded with Him, "Sir, do come down before my child dies!" Jesus said to him, "Go; your son lives!"

> The man believed what Jesus said to him and started home. As he was already going down the road, his servants met him and reported that his son was living and was healthy. So, he asked them at what time he began to get better. They said, "Yesterday during the seventh hour the fever left him." Then the father realized that it was at that very hour when Jesus had said to him, "Your son lives;" and he and his entire household believed and confidently trusted in Him as

Savior. This is the second miracle that Jesus performed in Cana after He had come from Judea to Galilee revealing that He is the Messiah. John 4:46-54

Commentary on this verse

The key to understanding this miracle is found in the geography. The nobleman and his dying son lived in Capernaum, the main city of the Galilee region. But Jesus was twenty miles away at Cana. That means a forty-mile round trip. The man made a two-day trek by foot to implore Jesus to heal His son. But Jesus merely spoke a word, producing results twenty miles away. No wonder the incident produced faith. Jesus is the master of distance.

> But when the unclean spirit has gone out of a man, it roams through dry [arid places] in search of rest, but it does not find any.
>
> Matthew 12:43

Chapter 6

Deliverance questions

Questions people have about deliverance.

1. What is a demon and where do they come from?

Demons are mentioned numerous times in the Bible. The Old Testament refers to them directly as "demons" (three times), "evil spirits" (eight times), or sometimes in a more obscure sense such as "prince" (in Daniel 10). The New Testament mentions demons many more times, calling them either "demons" (daimónion) or "evil spirits" over eighty times. The origin of demons is not explicitly addressed in Scripture.

Demon; an evil spirit, a source or agent of evil, harm, distress, or ruin. Many Christians believe that demons are fallen angels, cast from heaven with satan. This is the Scripture some use to identify demons as fallen angels.

> *And the great dragon was thrown down, that ancient serpent, who is called the devil and Satan, the deceiver of the whole world—he was thrown down to the earth, and his angels were thrown down with him.*
> *Revelation 12:9 ESV*

There are many who disagree. It is up to each individual to make that decision if they are interested. Regardless of a person's opinion of whether they are fallen angels or not, they are here from wherever they came from. I will include a few definitions from both views.

There is not one Scripture that describes what a demon looks like. They are a spirit of some kind but don't have their own bodies. This makes them disembodied spirits. Maybe that was their judgment for following satan in his fall.

Jesus said in Luke 24:39,

> Look at [the marks in] My hands and My feet, [and see] that it is I Myself. Touch Me and see; a spirit does not have flesh and bones, as you see that I have."

Scriptures says angels and demons are different.

> No, in all these things we are more than conquerors through him who loved us. For I am convinced that neither death nor life, neither angels nor demons, neither the present nor the future, nor any powers, neither height nor depth, nor anything else in all creation, will be able to separate us from the love of God that is in Christ Jesus our Lord."
> Romans 8:37–39 NIV

These verses are about the victory Christ has won over all the forces ranged against us. We are "more than conquerors" because no force—not life, not death, not angels, not demons, indeed nothing—can separate us from the love of God.

The "powers" referred to here are those with miraculous powers, whether false teachers and prophets or the very demonic entities that empower them. What is clear is that whoever they are, they cannot separate us from the love of God. Victory is assured!

Some sources suggest that the demons are the children of the rebellious angels that came to earth and cohabited with women and had children.

Where they came from might be a question that we never get answered, but what matters is that we understand these demonic spiritual entities are real, and they are our enemy.

It's up to us to do everything within ourselves to make them unwelcome in our lives and, if they are in us, to cast them out.

Angels

The definition of an angel is different than that of a demon.

Angel: a spiritual being serving as a divine messenger and intermediary and often as a special protector of an individual or nation. The word angel is derived from the Greek word *Angelos* and is the equivalent of the Hebrew word *mal'akh,* meaning "messenger.

Angels have bodies. They don't seek to inhabit a person or animal. Angels were created by God and there is no place in the Bible that says an angel would rather inhabit someone's body.

They are spiritual beings with their own bodies.

> *And it happened, as they were greatly perplexed about this, that behold, two men stood by them in shining garments. Then, as they were afraid and bowed their faces to the earth, they said to them, "Why do you seek the living among the dead? Luke 24:4-5 NKJV*

Every Scripture that speaks of an angel appearing to men has been described as looking like a man. The angel Gabriel appeared to Mary to announce that she would be the mother of the Son of God, and she replied, *"May it be done to me according to your word." (Luke 1:38)* The angels were messengers of God and conveyed God's will, and both Joseph and Mary trusted God and obeyed.

2. Do demons have bodies?

They are not like the angels who have their own bodies and who are not seeking to inhabit a human. Demons require and crave a host body to live in.

I have heard demons referred to as disembodied spirits. *Disembodied* - separated from or existing without the body. They do not like being out of a body, or a house, as they call it. They think that the house/body they reside in belongs to them. They are willing to share their home with fellow demons.

> *And he asked him, what is your name? And he answered, saying, my name is Legion: for we are many. Mark 5:9 NKJV*

After getting evicted, according to the Bible demons think to themselves, "If I go back and have a tough time getting back into my old house, I will bring some other demons and surely one of us is sure to find a way back in, then we will have a complete takeover."

Jesus reaffirmed this in Matthew 12:43-45.

> *When an unclean spirit comes out of a man, it passes through arid places seeking rest and does not find it. Then it says, 'I will return to the house I left.' On its return, it finds the house vacant, swept clean, and put in order. Then it goes and brings with it seven other spirits more wicked than itself, and they go in and dwell there, and the final plight of that man is worse than the first. So will it be with this wicked generation." (NIV)*

This is a warning that after we get delivered to be on the alert in every area of our lives. Because you may be guarding one door, but they may find entrance through a different door that had been left open in your life. By reading the Word, believing what it says, developing our relationship with Jesus, and praying daily we can easily stay clean.

3. Where do we send demons when we evict them?

Jesus is our example. There is only one Scripture where Jesus gave demons permission to go to a certain place when they came out of the man, and that was into a herd of pigs.

There is no scriptural validation to command demons to go anyplace when they leave a person.

Jesus said in Matthew 12:43,

> But when the unclean spirit has gone out of a man, it roams through dry [arid places] in search of rest, but it does not find any.

The Scripture does not tell us to send them to the pit, or to the foot of the cross, or to the Abyss, as I have heard some instruct demons. Because there aren't any scriptural instructions of where to direct them to go while they are being delivered, I wonder if the demons must pay attention to directions of where to go, or if they just go to dry places if they can't find a new home right away.

4. Do demons know who we are?

This next Scripture validates how demons recognize believers, and they are happy to give you their opinion. They knew who Jesus was.

> They went across the lake to the region of the Gerasene's. When Jesus got out of the boat, a man with an impure spirit came from the tombs to meet him. This man lived in the tombs, and no one could bind him anymore, not even with a chain. For he had often been chained hand and foot, but he tore the chains apart and broke the irons on his feet. No one was strong enough to subdue him. Night and day among the tombs and in

53

the hills, he would cry out and cut himself with stones. When he saw Jesus from a distance, he ran and fell on his knees in front of him. He shouted at the top of his voice, "What do you want with me, Jesus, Son of the Highest God? In God's name don't torture me!" For Jesus had said to him, "Come out of this man, you impure spirit!" Mark 5:1-8 NIV

While curing the sick, Jesus was approached by demons, who called out:

"You are the Son of God!" Jesus rebuked them and ordered them not to speak because they knew He was the Messiah. Luke 4:41 NIV

And immediately there was in their synagogue a man with an unclean spirit. And he cried out, "What have you to do with us, Jesus of Nazareth? Have you come to destroy us? I know who you are—the Holy One of God." Mark 1:24 ESV

They knew who the disciples were.

One day as we were going to the place of prayer, we were met by a slave girl with a spirit of divination, who earned a large income for her masters by fortune-telling. This girl followed Paul and the rest of us, shouting, "These men are servants of the Most High God, who are proclaiming to you the way of salvation. Acts 16:16-17 NLT

They will recognize us and our authority as believers. Most deliverance ministers have had demons say to them; "I know who you are." Along with that piece of information, it helps to know that they understand why you are there. They are about to be evicted!

5. What happens if the person performing the deliverance doesn't have a personal relationship with Jesus and is using their position of authority in a church to attempt to evict a demon?

There were some sons of the High priest in Israel. They were corrupt. They were professional exorcists who cast demons out of people. The Scripture isn't clear how they did this, but I can guess that they used the name of Beelzebub since they weren't working for God. This would be an example of the lying signs and wonders the Word speaks about.

The sons of Eli "knew not the Lord." 1 Samuel 2:12

In 1 Samuel 2:12, they are referred to as "sons of Belial", which is a term of derision used elsewhere in the Scriptures. The word Belial basically means "wickedness" or "worthlessness."

These men had heard of how the disciple named Paul was delivering people of demons using the name of Jesus and they were curious, and most likely jealous, probably because of their possible future loss of income.

Their dad was in the position of the highest religious leader (a high priest) in the kingdom. That relationship may have gained them some customers. Most likely they were being paid for their services and had been apparently casting the demons out at least temporarily by the authority of Beelzebub.

The demon in the man that they were attempting to cast out of got so mad at them for casting him out in the name of Jesus, that he jumped on all of them and took his rage out on them. The demon was able to do this because they weren't under the protection of Jesus like the believer is.

But...they got the surprise of their lives.

Then some of the itinerant Jewish exorcists undertook to invoke the name of the Lord Jesus over those who had evil spirits, saying, "I adjure you by the Jesus whom Paul proclaims." Seven sons of a Jewish high priest named Sceva were doing this. But the evil spirit answered them, "Jesus I know, and Paul I recognize, but who are you?" And the man in whom was the evil spirit leaped on them, mastered all of them and overpowered them so that they fled out of that house naked and wounded. Acts 19:13-16 ESV

The demons know Jesus and they had heard of Paul. Demons recognize those who are in relationship with Jesus and carry the true authority of Jesus Christ within them, and they knew that these men didn't have the authority to use the name of Jesus. Demons are physically stronger than men. Only God is stronger than the demons. John wrote,

The one who is in us is greater than the one who is in the world. 1 John 4:4b

Our strength is totally in the authority of Jesus living within us and in our relationship with Him.

6. Will they try to come back and get into us?

The Bible says yes. Jesus said in Luke 11:24-26,

When an unclean spirit goes out of a man, he goes through dry places, seeking rest; and finding none, he says, 'I will return to my house from which I came.' And when he comes, he finds it swept and put in order. Then he goes and takes with him seven other spirits more wicked than himself, and they enter and dwell there; and the last state of that man is worse than the first." (NKJV)

The *house* signifies our bodies. When someone has been delivered of a demon or demons, they got their house cleaned out. To keep demons from coming back, our house must be filled with the Word of God, which invites the presence of God and the Holy Spirit. Scripture also refers to our body as being a temple.

Do you not know that your body is a temple of the Holy Spirit who is within you, whom you have [received as a gift] from God and that you are not your own [property]? 1 Corinthians 6:19

Demons have a job to do, which is to try to get back into the house. Our job is to be prepared for their return and tell them the place they got kicked out of is not available. This would most likely be in the form of temptations that in the past we might have opened the door to them. Now that we have been cleaned out, we recognize those old temptations and slam the door in their face.

We do not need to be afraid of demons returning to us seeking a way to get into our house. Knowing what the Word says about what to expect empowers us. When the person is prepared, and the demon comes knocking and trying to get back in, the answer to the issue is "No, you can't come back. There is no vacancy!"

7. How can we spiritually prepare our house after we evict the demons from it?

We ask the Holy Spirit to come and fill every area of our bodies our minds, will, and emotions, and ask Him to lead guide, and direct us. We turn our lives over to Jesus. We read or listen to the Bible every day. We fill ourselves with the water of the Word. Fill up every dry place within ourselves. The Holy Spirit is a well of living water that continually springs up within us.

...but whoever drinks of the water that I will give him shall never thirst, but the water that I will give him will

become in him a well of water springing up to eternal life. John 4:14 NKJV

The Word of God is a symbol of cleansing water.

Husbands, love your wives, just as Christ loved the church and gave Himself up for her to sanctify her, cleansing her by the washing with water through the word. Ephesians 5:25-26 NKJV

As we fill ourselves with the water of the Word the demons won't find any entrance open that they can come in.

8. Can a person who has a demon deliver another person of a demon?

Through observation and personal experience, I have seen deliverance ministers operate successfully to deliver other believers of demons when they themselves had some demonic influences within themselves. Many of us have areas in our lives that have not come under the complete control of the Holy Spirit.

It is possible to be in the dark about the fact that a person has a demon hiding within their personality. On the other hand, I have had people who told me they were aware that they were captive in some area of their life and that maybe a demon was involved, but they were not ready to deal with it yet.

That did not stop them from ministering deliverance to someone who needed it, and those they ministered to were able to receive their deliverance. I know that some ministers might not agree with that, but I don't say this as my opinion, I have seen it through experience. It is a mystery that we may not understand, but God extends His grace to those who are not ready to be delivered and does not reject them from helping others.

If we had to be perfect before we could help others, nothing would get done for the Kingdom of God. We are human volunteers for Jesus, and we are all a work in progress. The Lord looks upon our hearts and helps us. Deliverance isn't successful in our human strength or power. We work under the designated authority of Jesus and His name. When Jesus was performing a deliverance, the demons spoke to Him and confirmed they knew they didn't have any place in Him.

At sunset, people brought to Jesus all who were sick. He placed his hands on each one and healed them. Also, demons came out of many people. The demons shouted, "You are the Son of God!" But he commanded them to be quiet. He would not allow them to speak, because they knew he was the Messiah.
Luke 4:40-41 NIV

The demons were very aware that they and Jesus belonged to two radically different kingdoms and had nothing in common. The demon was speaking for all the demons who were inside the person.

There is a good possibility that if a person is casting a demon out of someone that they themselves struggle with, the demon might just accuse them in front of others of having a demon inside of them and it could be embarrassing. But it doesn't change the fact that Jesus is the one doing the delivering. The minister who is a believer is just the facilitator. The Lord knows the timing for the minister who needs to be set free. It's not up to anyone to judge.

Paul struggled with the sin nature within himself but was able to minister to others despite it.

I love God's law with all my heart. But there is another power within me that is at war with my mind. This power makes me a slave to the sin that is still within

59

me. Oh, what a miserable person I am! Who will free me from this life that is dominated by sin and death?"
Romans 7:22-24 NLT

9. Should we allow demons to talk with us when we are performing deliverance?

I have heard people say to not ever let a demon speak when you are performing deliverance. Opinions vary as to the answer to this question.

There are several places in Scripture where Jesus had a conversation with the demons. The demons asked him questions and he responded by asking them a question. They knew they would have to leave and could not stay.

They went across the lake to the region of the Gerasenes. When Jesus got out of the boat, a man with an impure spirit came from the tombs to meet him. This man lived in the tombs, and no one could bind him anymore, not even with a chain. For he had often been chained hand and foot, but he tore the chains apart and broke the irons on his feet. No one was strong enough to subdue him. Night and day among the tombs and in the hills, he would cry out and cut himself with stones.

When he saw Jesus from a distance, he ran and fell on his knees in front of him. He shouted at the top of his voice, "What do you want with me, Jesus, Son of the Highest God? In God's name don't torture me!" For Jesus had said to him, "Come out of this man, you impure spirit!"

Then Jesus asked him, "What is your name?" "My name is Legion," he replied, "for we are many." And he begged Jesus repeatedly not to send them out of the area.

*A large herd of pigs was feeding on the nearby hillside.
The demons begged Jesus, "Send us among the pigs;
allow us to go into them." He gave them permission,
and the impure spirits came out and went into the pigs.
The herd, about two thousand in number, rushed down
the steep bank into the lake and were drowned.*

*Those tending the pigs ran off and reported this in the
town and countryside, and the people went out to see
what had happened. When they came to Jesus, they
saw the man who had been possessed by the legion of
demons, sitting there, dressed and in his right mind;
and they were afraid. Those who had seen it told the
people what had happened to the demon-possessed
man—and talked about the pigs as well. Then the
people began to plead with Jesus to leave their region.
Mark 5:1-16 NIV*

From this Scripture, it does not seem that demons are fussy
about what type of body they inhabit. These demons begged
Jesus to let them go into the pigs and He agreed to their
request. The pigs had a definite reaction when the demons
entered them, and in their panic and fear, they ran into the
sea and drowned.

Why did the people beg Jesus to leave the area? You would
think they would be glad for the demon-possessed man to be
set free and welcome Jesus into their area. I have heard it
explained that when they lost the pigs, they lost their income,
so they did not want Jesus to stay in the area in case He
caused more problems like this for other pig farmers. Another
opinion is that some of the demons went into the people after
they left the pigs, which made the people afraid of Jesus, so
they begged Him to leave the area.

Even though the pigs perished, the demons did not. Demons
do not die. They just look for another home.

61

10. If a demon talks, what might he say?

Some say demons are ignorant. Some of the things they might say can sound dumb to us, but they are not stupid. They are prideful, just like their father satan. They may begin to talk to you once they figure out you have the authority to make them leave, and you intend to do that. They may start a "Let's make a deal" conversation.

They will plead and whine and sometimes manifest with crying. If that does not work, they may get belligerent and say they will not leave, and you cannot make them. Do not be surprised at anything they might say to you as the deliverance minister. They may threaten you. They cannot hurt you, so you do not need to be afraid. They are afraid.

They will blame each other if they think they can divert the attention off themselves and get you to leave them alone. They may tell you that you need to get the others out because the other demons are the ones who cause the host so much trouble.

They operate in confusion and lies. Sometimes they will begin to fight amongst themselves, which you can witness. The person might just sit quietly while this is all going on, even though the demons are using their mouth. As ridiculous as this might sound, it's true. It would be wise if you are called on to pray for someone to be delivered to be prepared for almost anything.

We usually tell demons they cannot manifest, but sometimes it can be good for a person to hear a demon manifest and speak out of their own mouth to believe they really have a demon. Once that happens and the deliverance follows, it's understandable why no one would ever convince them that a Christian cannot have a demon. Experience will trump opinion every time.

If allowed to speak, they may say things such as, "You cannot help him or her," or say, "They belong to me." The main goal of the demon is to hang on to their victim and to make you believe you have no authority over them. Tell them to be quiet in the name of Jesus.

Before we begin, we usually address the demon by saying to the person that we are going to take care of every spiritual legal right a demon might have to inhabit the person. Then we lead the person in a prayer of repentance and forgiveness for any sin they have committed against God or His Word and any generational sin. This makes it easier to get the demons out because they don't have any legal right to cling to.

Jesus is the only true deliverer.
He promises us that He can deliver us.

> And it shall come to pass that whosoever shall call on
> the name of the LORD shall be delivered.
> Joel. 2:32a NKJV

You may encounter Christians who have consulted a medium when they could not get help from the church.

> Do not turn to mediums or necromancers; do not seek
> them out, and so make yourselves unclean by them: I
> am the Lord your God. Leviticus 19:31 ESV

People get desperate. If someone you are ministering to shares that they have tried to get help from the occult, do not judge them. It's important to explain to them that consulting with a medium or a witch is the same as consulting with satan. Explain how they will need to repent and ask forgiveness for doing that in their ignorance, because it's possible one or more demons used that open door as an opportunity to enter in. If a person did this, it would open the door, particularly to an unclean spirit.

"Someone may say to you, 'Let us ask the mediums and those who consult the spirits of the dead. With their whisperings and mutterings, they will tell us what to do.' But shouldn't people ask God for guidance?"
Isaiah 8:19 NLT

11. How do I know if I need deliverance?

One sign that you may be dealing with a demon is that demons compel people to do things that are negative to their lives. When a person has a problem controlling their negative impulses, a demon could be at work. Is there a recurring pattern in your life that is harmful or destructive such as poverty, drinking, fighting, infirmity, fear, etc.? Pray and ask the Lord to show you if a demon could be at work that you need to be delivered from.

12. Can a demon make me sick?

Is all sickness rooted in a curse or a demon? I am not saying that every infirmity that a person deals with is a demon. There is one case in the Bible as an example for us that shows us a demon or sin is not always the cause of infirmity.

His disciples asked him, "Rabbi, who sinned, this man or his parents, that he was born blind?" "Neither this man nor his parents sinned," said Jesus, "but this happened so that the works of God might be displayed in him.
John 9:1-3 NIV

At the same time, Jesus did not deny that demons cause health issues. In this case, it was not the result of their work. Some illnesses or infirmities are brought on by practical means. It can come from the way a person feeds themselves. When we abuse our bodies with overindulgence of food, too much sugar, lack of sleep, lack of exercise or other negative behaviors and habits they can be the root cause of health issues. The body responds and is influenced by how we take care of ourselves. If we do not take care of ourselves our health will pay the price, but it does not always mean the person has a demon.

13. Do demons always manifest during deliverance?

Not always. If you go through the deliverance session and not one demon manifests, don't think that they haven't been evicted. We have this example from the Bible that a woman had suffered for eighteen years from a spirit of infirmity. When Jesus delivered her there wasn't a peep from the demon, but it was cast out.

> On a Sabbath Jesus was teaching in one of the synagogues, and a woman was there who had been crippled by a spirit for eighteen years. She was bent over and could not straighten up at all. When Jesus saw her, he called her forward and said to her, "Woman, you are set free from your infirmity." Then he put his hands on her, and immediately she straightened up and praised God.
>
> Indignant because Jesus had healed on Sabbath, the synagogue ruler said to the people, "There are six days for work. So, come and be healed on those days, not on the Sabbath." Jesus answered him: "You hypocrites! Doesn't each one of you on the Sabbath untie his ox or donkey from the stall and lead it out to give it water? Then should not this woman, a daughter of Abraham, whom Satan has kept bound for eighteen long years, be set free on the Sabbath day from what bound her?" Luke 13:10-16 NIV

There are several things to note with this Scripture besides the demon leaving without a fuss. For the woman to be healed of her infirmity, the demon had to be cast out. After the deliverance, Jesus laid hands on her for healing, and she was healed. How many people are not being healed because of a demon within them preventing it?

Jesus called this woman a daughter of Abraham and she was in the synagogue on the Sabbath. That means she was a believer in God. She wasn't a random person who wandered in off the street. It was important to the religious leaders that one of their own hadn't been set free and suffered so many years. They may have prayed for deliverance for her before but didn't have the authority, even as priests, to deliver her. It took Jesus -- and they couldn't comprehend this.

Unfortunately, we find this to be quite common in many denominational churches today. Pastors aren't taught deliverance in most seminaries. Many people try everything to be healed, but until they receive deliverance they stay plagued with the problems which could stem from demons. The demons block their healing.

Recently, a professional counselor I know asked me if I would come and pray with a man who had been in counseling for years. She said that he had issues in his life that, even after many years he hadn't been able to overcome. He had a history of being ministered to by different qualified people and had become very discouraged. She had been ministering to him for about a year. In one session he said to her; "I think maybe I have a demon and that's why I haven't been able to overcome my issues."

I agreed to pray with them. There were three of us taking him through deliverance. We went through the whole session, and he never saw one thing or felt anything leave. I had never had this happen. After evicting each strongman and the demons under him, before we moved on to the next one, I would ask him if he felt anything leave. He would say, "No, but I feel much lighter inside." When we were finished, we thanked the Lord for his complete healing and total freedom from all bondages. He said he felt much better and left. We discussed amongst ourselves this highly unusual session. Not one demon manifested itself. We were all skeptical of the man's complete deliverance and healing.

I spoke with the counselor a week after his next session and she said when the man returned for his next counseling appointment, he was so excited to report that the deliverance had set him completely free. After a few months, he was able to stop going to counseling and is truly a changed person, after years of counseling with many different people to no avail. It was sad that, in all the years, no one had offered him deliverance. We wouldn't expect worldly non-Christian counselors to offer it, but he had also gone to many Christian counselors.

Hosea 4:6 says, *My people are destroyed due to lack of knowledge.* And that is surely the truth when it comes to deliverance. When He says, "My people" He means believers, not worldly people. As believers, it's our responsibility to be equipped and train all other believers to take people through deliverance so they don't spiritually perish because of some demons in them.

14. What if a person isn't saved, but needs deliverance?

There may be some who are reading this who will immediately think of people who they feel need deliverance, and this information would help them. But if the person they are concerned about is not a believer they would not understand this subject and might become offended or think you are crazy. Pray for their salvation, along with a true born-again experience, so they can receive this truth and hopefully get the deliverance they need.

As the bird by wandering,

as the swallow by flying,

so the curse causeless

shall not come.

Proverbs 26:2 KJV

Chapter 7

Ways demons can enter a person

Demons are continually looking for open doors so they can gain access to enter people. There are many ways a demon might find a door into a person. An open door can come through any sin a person, or someone in their generational bloodline, has committed.

In the case of a generational bloodline curse, a demon can enter the person while they are in their mother's womb. In cases where a demon has lodged itself within the generational bloodline, it isn't anything the person has done wrong, but they pay the consequences.

> *The Lord...visits the iniquity of the fathers on the children and the children's children, to the third and the fourth generation. Exodus 34:6-7 NKJV*

One of the sins that will allow demons to get into generational bloodlines is if their ancestors have worshipped foreign gods.

> *You shall not make for yourself a carved image—any likeness of anything that is in heaven above, or that is in the earth beneath, or that is in the water under the earth; you shall not bow down to them nor serve them. Deuteronomy 5:8–9a NKJV*

A New Testament Scripture concerning the generational bloodline and demons is found in John 9:1-3:

> *While He was passing by, He noticed a man [who had been] blind from birth. His disciples asked Him, "Rabbi*

(Teacher), who sinned, this man or his parents, that he would be born blind?" Jesus answered, "Neither this man nor his parents sinned, but it was so that the works of God might be displayed and illustrated in him.

The religious Jews of Jesus' day knew the warnings the Old Testament gave concerning demons and generational sins.

Because of their iniquity, and also because of the iniquities of their fathers they shall rot away like them. Leviticus 26:39 ESV

Iniquity refers to a premeditated choice. To commit iniquity is to continue without repentance. God forgives iniquity, as He does any type of sin, when we repent.

Now repent of your sins and turn to God, so that your sins may be wiped away. Acts 3:19 NLT

Sin means "to miss the mark." The sin nature is present in every human being born since the fall of Adam. Our sinful nature causes us to gravitate naturally toward selfishness, envy, and pride, even when we are trying to do good.

When Adam sinned, sin entered the world. Adam's sin brought death, so death spread to everyone, for everyone sinned. Romans 5:12 NLT

The spirit of fear, or any other demon, can get itself assigned to a curse against the bloodline, because of some sin or iniquity committed against the Lord by an ancestor. This gives it a doorway to enter the person. If a strongman of fear is in a mother and enters into a child she is carrying, then the child will also struggle with fear until they get deliverance.

If a person experiences a traumatic incident a demon can enter at that time, especially a demon of fear. If there was shock or trauma involved, they are demons too.

In my case, I believe fear entered me as a teenager after watching some scary movies at a friend's house and then walking/running in fear to my home after dark. The Bible talks about other root causes that give demons legal rights to be inside a person.

Sin and iniquity gain their authority by using the laws of God against us.

Demons usually get into people through sin or curses. That is the argument of defense they use in the Courtroom of Heaven. God must judge sin, so when a person sins the devil takes advantage of that provision of God's law to use in the Courtroom of Heaven against them.

For us to rebuke a demon or attempt to deliver a person who has a guilty charge of sin against them will not work. The sin must be repented for and forgiven. Then God is able to use His power and authority to set the person free.

As we study God's Word, we learn that everything is about authority and legal rights in the spiritual kingdom, just as it is in the physical realm. On earth when we break the law and are caught, we face the consequences. We must pay the price determined by the court.

The Bible says in 1 Corinthians 15:56b: *The strength of sin is the law. (NKJV)*

What is the law? It's God's Word, the Scriptures. If we as believers have any unconfessed sin, then we do not have the full legal rights of liberation. Satan still has a legal claim against us. He is a legalist and knows his rights before God to send demons into a person. Learn to think of Satan as a lawyer demanding his rights before God. The name of satan is a title, Ha-satan. In Hebrew, it means 'prosecuting attorney'.

Scripture defines sin as lawlessness.

Everyone who sins breaks the law; in fact, sin is lawlessness. 1 John 3:4 NIV

The evil deeds of the wicked ensnare them; the cords of their sins hold them fast. Proverbs 5:22 NIV

These cords created through sin aren't only for the wicked. They ensnare believers too. Believers who have sinned or have active sin in their lives become targets for judgment. It does not matter to the devil or a demon if you are a believer or not. He rejoices if he can capture a believer. The unbeliever is already his captive. Unforgiveness gives a demon a legal right to enter a person.

And when you stand praying, if you hold anything against anyone, forgive them, so that your Father in heaven may forgive you your sins." Mark 11:25 NIV

Forgiveness is the remedy.

And be ye kind one to another, tenderhearted, forgiving one another, even as God for Christ's sake hath forgiven you. Ephesians 4:32 KJV

I have heard that unforgiveness towards someone is like a person drinking poison and expecting the other person to die. Unforgiveness hurts us, not the other person. Anger and bitterness are spiritual relatives to unforgiveness and usually come in at the same time. They work together to put us into captivity. We tend to focus on what gave us that justification for unforgiveness, and we might not understand that we are opening a door to a prison cell to bondage if we don't forgive.

For I see that you are full of bitterness and captive to sin. Acts 8:23 NIV

The Bible says that with a cause that could be a spiritual legal right, a curse can settle on a person. Demons are attached to these curses and utilize the legal right to torment people and keep them in captivity.

> *As the bird by wandering, as the swallow by flying, so the curse causeless shall not come. Proverbs 26:2 KJV*

A curse, like a demon, does not just land on us without a reason. Behind every curse that comes upon us, there is a cause. A legal cause in the spiritual courtroom of heaven.

> *Be angry [at sin—at immorality, at injustice, at ungodly behavior], yet do not sin; do not let your anger [cause you shame, nor allow it to] last until the sun goes down. And do not give the devil an opportunity [to lead you into sin by holding a grudge, or nurturing anger, or harboring resentment, or cultivating bitterness]. Ephesians 4:26-27*

Another possibility of a root cause might be a demon who gained legal rights during a person's worldly sinful life before accepting Christ. Some people have been abused emotionally and physically, which may have opened doors for demons to come in and torment them. If they didn't receive deliverance when they got saved, then the demon is still there. They don't leave without being cast out.

This could also be compared to getting a thorn in your foot. If the thorn is not removed, it is going to cause problems. The longer it stays in a person's foot, the bigger the problem will be. The wound will begin to fester and get infected. This will surely affect a person's walk. The thorn is not going to leave by itself. It must be identified and removed.

The solution is to pray a prayer of repentance on behalf of sin committed against the Lord by our generational bloodline or by us. When we ask forgiveness, it erases any legal right a curse has to operate. Then, it is necessary to cast out any demons that may be attached to the curse and decree an infilling of healing to fill the vacated space.

Every believer already has the victory over every demon, as long as this rule that has been laid out in the Scriptures is followed, which is repentance for sins and asking for forgiveness, then turning from your wicked way and walking God's way. Demons are afraid that we will discover them and evict them in the name of Jesus—it is as simple as that.

It helps to understand that demons are just doing their job. Their boss is the devil. He assigns them to unsuspecting victims who have opened doors in their lives that allow the demons to enter. It is our job as disciples of Christ to prevent them from doing what they want to do to us, which is to make our lives miserable. We do that by casting them out when we discover them.

In the story of Job, the devil couldn't find a way to get to Job because he was under God's protection. He was righteous, so God had a protective fence around him. (Job 1:10)

It's the same for us if we are clean before the Lord. If adversity occurs and you have done everything you know to do to be a righteous servant before the Lord, then it could be happening for a testimony that will give God the Glory. As humans, we don't always understand the ways of God. In the story of Joseph, he went through so many trials and ended up in prison, but never blamed God for his misfortune. In the end, God elevated him from being a slave to becoming the second most powerful man in Egypt. (Genesis 37-50)

Chapter 8

Practical aspects of deliverance

Usually, when a person decides they need deliverance it becomes an urgent matter to them, and they want to get it done right now. This person may put pressure on the person that is going to take them through deliverance to arrange a meeting as soon as they can. Sometimes a person expects them to drop everything they are currently busy with and meet with them.

The person who is facilitating the deliverance does not need to drop everything and set aside other obligations or scheduled family commitments if a person calls and says they need deliverance right away.

The way the deliverance minister responds to the person is, of course, up to them, and there are times when it may need to be done quickly. Although there can be benefits to putting it on hold for a few days. It may be frustrating, but doing it this way will give time for the person who is receiving deliverance to fast and pray. What seems to be a delay is really a valuable time of preparation.

The extra time gives the Lord time to reveal more to the person concerning how this demon has affected their thoughts and actions in negative ways. They can ask the Lord to reveal the names of the demons that need to be evicted, which is always helpful. The time they take to prepare themselves will help them to look forward to being set free, and they will come to their deliverance meeting strong in spirit.

Another recommendation would be to suggest they take communion every day before the deliverance session, and even a few days after, thanking the Lord for the covenant they have with Him and that they have been bought and paid for by the blood of Jesus Christ.

Unless the Holy Spirit tells a person to come to a deliverance session in a fasting state, they should not come with their stomach growling and their mind telling them they are hungry; this is distracting. Some people feel that they need to be in a fasting state for the deliverance. This is up to the individual person.

As the deliverance minister, if I am going to fast and pray, it will be for a day or so *before* I minister – as a preparation. I know many refer to the Scripture where Jesus told the disciples that demons would only come out by prayer and fasting.

> *However, this kind does not go out except by prayer and fasting. Matthew 17:21 NKJV*

He didn't say when we need to fast before performing the deliverance. He was implying that they needed to have a fasting lifestyle so they would be spiritually ready at any time to perform any type of deliverance that might be needed. Jesus lived a fasting lifestyle.

There are many ways to fast other than food. Jesus speaks of a fast that will set people free from the bondage that comes from sin if they will do as the Word says.

> *[Rather] is this, not the fast which I choose, to undo the bonds of wickedness, to tear to pieces the ropes of the yoke, To let the oppressed go free And break apart every [enslaving] yoke? "Is it not to divide your bread with the hungry and bring the homeless poor into the*

76

house; When you see the naked, that you cover him, and not to hide from [the needs of] your own flesh and blood?

Then your light will break out like the dawn, and your healing (restoration, new life) will quickly spring forth; Your righteousness will go before you [leading you to peace and prosperity], The glory of the Lord will be your rear guard. Then you will call, and the Lord will answer; You will cry for help, and He will say, 'Here I am.'

Next is the condition that needs to be met to obtain the promise.

If you take away from your midst the yoke [of oppression], The finger pointed in scorn [toward the oppressed or the godly], and [every form of] wicked (sinful, unjust) speech, and if you offer yourself to [assist] the hungry and satisfy the need of the afflicted.

Then your light will rise in the darkness and your gloom will become like midday. "And the Lord will continually guide you, and satisfy your soul in scorched and dry places, and give strength to your bones, and you will be like a watered garden and like a spring of water whose waters do not fail. "And your people will rebuild the ancient ruins; You will raise up and restore the age-old foundations [of buildings that have been laid waste]; You will be called Repairer of the Breach, Restorer of Streets with Dwellings. Isaiah 48:6-12

I have always thought that this 'repairer of the breach' of the ancient ruins of many generations included our generational bloodlines. Because of sin, the curse has entered. When we repent, we close that breach between our generational bloodline and God. And He can rebuild and repair. Of course, it could also mean geographical locations, but we can bring freedom in this way to our ancient bloodlines.

We can turn this Scripture into a powerful decree to speak over ourselves of what God will do for us after repenting of our sins.

Another thing we can do while preparing for deliverance

A powerful weapon to use while preparing for deliverance is self-talk. This can be done out loud or to yourself about the upcoming deliverance. Decree things like:

Thank You, Jesus, for setting me free. The blood of Jesus paid the price for my freedom, and by His stripes, I am healed. I am going to be a totally new creation, body, soul, and spirit. Any demonic spirits within me are going to leave me completely!

This is prophesying the end from the beginning. When the person has been speaking over themselves about their soon coming freedom, it usually makes the deliverance go much easier and quicker.

> *Declaring the end from the beginning and from ancient times the things that are not yet done, saying, my counsel shall stand, and I will do all my pleasure.*
> *Isaiah 46:10 NKJV*

The Lord takes great pleasure in setting His people free from all bondages.

Demons manifesting

Share with the person that sometimes the demons may manifest as they are getting ready to come for deliverance. This could be in different ways, such as giving their host a headache or a stomachache. The closer the time gets for their deliverance session, the more intense things can become.

When the person has been instructed ahead of time that this may happen, and it does, it reinforces that they are on the right path. They can bind the demon that is giving them the headache or stomach issues.

They don't have to know its name, but if the Holy Spirit reveals the name to them, they can use its name and say, "*In the name of Jesus, headache (or name the spirit) be bound, you cannot manifest in me. I loose myself from you in the name of Jesus.*"When a person realizes the battle is internal, in their mind, they can be encouraged that they are going to have a victory soon.

The demons may not manifest at all, but that doesn't mean they aren't there. We have found that they strategize too. They want to convince a person they really aren't there. It just depends on which strategy they think will work the best for them.

It is good to know that if a person wants deliverance badly enough, they will not let anything get in the way of receiving their deliverance. It is not up to anyone to try to convince or talk a person into deliverance. If they ask, just give them the information concerning deliverance and let the Holy Spirit work in the situation.

If a person has a strong addiction, no matter how people try to influence them, a person cannot break their addiction until they make up their own mind that they don't want it anymore. If they decide to do it for someone else, like a spouse or children, usually it will not work. They need a heart change; they can ask God to help them with that.

They must see for themself what it is doing to them and begin to hate the addiction to be able to receive their deliverance and truly be set free. Demons know if the person really wants to get rid of them or not. As stated before, demons won't leave a person on their own. They must be cast out.

If the demons are strong in a person, the person may back out the first time. It is hard to release that hope that they were going to be set free if you know they really need the deliverance. But the Holy Spirit will do that work, and when they are ready they will truly get their deliverance. They have a better chance of staying free because they make the decision to be set free with a strong desire in their spirit that outweighs their flesh.

Prepare yourself for the deliverance

Prepare yourself to stay neutral and confident. Even if you are a little nervous the first few times, it helps to know the demons cannot read your mind. We have had demons stare at us out of the eyes of the person we are ministering to as we are explaining to the person how the deliverance is going to go. It usually is a look of hatred or fear, or one then the other.

Even if a person spits or takes a swing at us, we have never been directly hit or hurt in any way.

> The seventy returned with joy, saying, "Lord, even the demons are subject to us in Your name." He said to them, "I watched satan fall from heaven like [a flash of] lightning. Listen carefully: I have given you authority [that you now possess] to tread on serpents and scorpions, and [the ability to exercise authority] over all the power of the enemy (satan); and nothing will [in any way] harm you. Luke 10:17-19

Performing deliverance on another person by yourself.

We do not recommend performing a deliverance on another person by yourself. This is not out of fear of the demonic, but it is important, from a legal standpoint, to have a witness to protect the one doing the deliverance. Of course, if you are good friends and it is a simple deliverance of one or two demons, and the person is a mature believer, that is another thing.

If a person you are going to minister to has told you, "I have had lots of prayer for this before," or, "I hear voices all the time telling me to kill myself," then it would be common sense to make an appointment to have at least one other person with you to pray with them since it could get complicated.

If you cannot complete the deliverance in one session, then schedule another session. Be sensitive to the person and how they seem to be doing. If they are getting tired, take a break and relax. Even set up another appointment.

In the early days of helping people get delivered, we used to pray with a person for two to four hours, or longer if needed. We thought that maybe if we took a break it would mess up the deliverance. If you are reading this and have been familiar with deliverance ministry, you will be able to relate to that. We know better now. The demons that have been delivered are gone and will not slip back in unless the person invites them in. The ones that are still there most likely have been there many years and aren't going anywhere. It's ok to take a break.

A deliverance session is confidential

The person getting a deliverance needs to be told that what goes on during their deliverance session is confidential. The only people who will have knowledge of what occurred during their ministry time will be whoever is present at the time. If they want to share their experience with someone else, that will be up to them.

How to calm a person concerning the unknown in deliverance

Explaining what may happen before beginning the deliverance helps people to feel prepared. Let them know that you can stop their deliverance at any time. Deliverance is not something that once you start you cannot stop.

The fear of the unknown is a powerful force especially if a person is dealing with a spirit of fear within them. It is always good to assure the person that Jesus and you are always in control during the deliverance, and they do not need to be afraid. When they know that you as the coach, and Jesus as their Deliverer, will not let the demon harm them, it will help erase any anxiety over their deliverance that they may have.

There can be a normal conversation during deliverance.

Explain to the person you are praying with that they can talk to you during their deliverance. They will not suddenly go deaf and dumb. If there are areas where the demon has had a lot of influence and control over the host person, you might find you are talking with the demon and must silence him to communicate with the person. The way you would do this is to say; "Be silent in the name of Jesus. I want to talk to ___."

The demon is listening to everything you are telling the person, so the more you talk about what Jesus is going to do for the person because He paid the price for their freedom at the cross, the more nervous and the less fight the demon will put up—if they do put up a fight. Assure the person that the Jesus in you and the Jesus in them is able to overcome every strongman or demon.

Then he answered and spoke unto me, saying, this is the word of the LORD to Zerubbabel, saying, not by might, nor by power, but by my spirit, says the LORD of hosts. Zechariah 4:6 NKJV

Sharing past experiences

Do not share past experiences with the person getting the deliverance if it could be something that would scare them. It could be tempting, if you have had interesting experiences with deliverance, to share some stories of what demons have said or done. Usually that would not be a good thing to do because you never know how the session is going to go. And remember, the demon is listening. If you tell stories of how demons manifested in other deliverances, they may copy that behavior and make it more time-consuming for you. The important thing is that you, as the person in charge, needs to be prepared.

Prepare the person concerning the different feelings they can feel physically during the deliverance. You could explain a few things that quite often occur during the deliverance process, such as they may feel demons begin to move around inside of them. They may feel them come up into their throat and they will feel the need to cough. Tell them that is a natural thing to happen, and the demon quite often leaves through coughing. Sometimes it is a good belch that evicts them. Always have a small wastebasket and a box of tissue handy in case it is needed, and the person gets rid of them by gagging, or throwing up or spitting them out.

The demons are helpless to do anything to hurt anyone because of Jesus in us. Demons have thrown people down on the floor as we ministered, but no one we have prayed with has ever been hurt in any way.

The demons threw a man down that Jesus was ministering deliverance to and it didn't hurt him.

But Jesus rebuked him, saying, "Be silent (muzzled, gagged) and come out of him!" And when the demon had thrown the man down among them, he came out of him without injuring him in any way. Luke 4:35

Chapter 9

The importance of identifying the Strongman

Or how can someone enter a strong man's house and plunder his goods, unless he first binds (ties up) the strong man? Then indeed he may plunder (ransack) his house. Matthew 12:29

When the Scriptures I am using speak of binding and loosing, they refer to the strongman who is guarding a stronghold in a human being. A strongman is also known as a "gatekeeper." He oversees the demons. He is the chief demon that is over other demons in a person's body.

The Bible refers to the body as a temple, tabernacle, or house.

When the strong man, fully armed, guards his own house, his belongings are undisturbed and secure. But when someone stronger than he attacks and overpowers him, he robs him of all his armor on which he had relied and divides his [goods as] spoil. Luke 11:21-22

An example of this armor that the strongman is armed with could be self-love, unbelief, and the lies that he can get the person to believe. The goods or spoil that he speaks of are the souls of men that are full of sinful motives and attitudes.

For though we walk in the flesh, we are not waging war according to the flesh. For the weapons of our warfare are not of the flesh but have divine power to destroy strongholds. 2 Corinthians 10:3-4 ESV

85

We defeat our enemy with spiritual weapons that remove all authority and power from the strongman and the demons under him. Our weapons are repentance, forgiveness, the Word of God, the blood of Jesus, and the word of our testimony. They are powerful enough to defeat every enemy we have.

A strongman guards his strongholds

The battlefield is fought in the mind of the victim. If the enemy can get the person to believe the lies that he tells him, then he wins the battle and secures his captive.

> *But I fear, lest somehow, as the serpent deceived Eve by his craftiness, so your minds may be corrupted from the simplicity that is in Christ. For if he who comes preaches another Jesus whom we have not preached, or if you receive a different spirit which you have not received or a different gospel which you have not accepted—you may well put up with it!*
> *2 Corinthians 11:3-4*

The apostle Paul is concerned that a believer may be fooled and believe lies from the enemy as Eve did, and in doing so will receive a different spirit, a spirit of deception. The accuser would then continue to lie to the person and lead them into bondage from that stronghold. A common saying is "If the devil can get a toehold, he will go for a foothold, and before long he will have a stronghold."

Identifying a strongman

There may be one, two, or many strongmen in a person. They each rule over their own area or domain in a person's soul realm. Most deliverance ministers know the best way to get demons out is to establish who the strongman over them is. When we bind and cast him out, then it's easier to get the demons that are under his authority out.

But no one can go into a strong man's house and steal his property unless he first overpowers and ties up the strong man, and then he will ransack and rob his house. Mark 3:27

It is clear in Scripture that when a person has a stronghold of sin in their soul, it becomes a fortress that the enemy has developed within them that protects him from being discovered. From this command center, the strongman strengthens his hold on a person. He summons his underlings, the demons, to come in and help him in the battle.

We explain to the person the key to successful deliverance is to repent for any sin they may have committed that has, and may still be, giving the demons the legal right to enter them. They need to repent and renounce the sin and ask for and receive forgiveness from God for that sin.

This will render the strongman powerless to stop the plundering of the host he is living in. As stated, before, he does not have a weapon that can fight against a person humbling themselves before God in repentance and asking forgiveness for the sins in their life.

Satan is a legalist. One of his names is 'the accuser.' As shared earlier, the name satan in the Hebrew language is a title. It is pronounced Ha-sa-tan. It means prosecuting attorney. As the prosecutor, he knows God's laws and will use them for his purposes to get a conviction against a person. He knows what is spiritually lawful for a believer and what is sin. Another word for sin is *lawlessness.*

Everyone who practices sin also practices lawlessness; and sin is lawlessness [ignoring God's law by action or neglect or by tolerating wrongdoing—being unrestrained by His commands and His will]. 1 John 3:4

When a person is born again into the Kingdom of God, they will not instantly have the revelation of what is scripturally lawful and pleasing to the Lord, and what is sin or lawlessness. They must be taught by those mature in the Word of God and learn by reading the Word.

Because of ignorance of the ways of God, a man perishes spiritually, which can also affect his children and they will pay the price for his sins.

> *My people are destroyed for lack of knowledge. Because you have rejected knowledge, I also will reject you from being My priest. Since you have forgotten the law of your God, I also will forget your children.*
> *Hosea 4:6 NKJV*

Chapter 10

Guide for group or self-deliverance

The deliverance session can be done as a group, self-deliverance, or a session with one or two facilitators. If you are considering doing a deliverance and have not experienced this before, it would be recommended that you find someone who is familiar with the process. If you can't find someone who is experienced, enlist a few other interested, mature Christians. Then, decide who among you will be leading the deliverance session.

The Scripture instructs us to test the spirits.

Beloved, do not put faith in every spirit, but prove (test) the spirits to discover whether they proceed from God; for many false prophets have gone forth into the world. By this you may know (perceive and recognize) the Spirit of God: every spirit which acknowledges and confesses [the fact] that Jesus Christ (the Messiah) [actually] has become man and has come in the flesh is of God [has God for its source]; And every spirit which does not acknowledge and confess that Jesus Christ has come in the flesh [but would annul, destroy, sever, disunite Him] is not of God [does not proceed from Him].

This [non-confession] is the [spirit] other antichrist, [of] which you heard that it was coming, and now it is already in the world. Little children, you are of God [you belong to Him] and have [already] defeated and overcome them [the agents of the antichrist], because

He Who lives in you is greater (mightier) than he who is in the world. 1 John 4:1-6

Additional information on generational bloodline curses.

In case someone is wondering why they should repent for those in their generational bloodline, here are some Scriptures.

The Lord is slow to anger and abundant in lovingkindness, forgiving iniquity and transgression; but He will by no means clear the guilty, visiting the iniquity of the fathers on the children to the third and the fourth generations. Numbers 14:18 ESV

If they confess their wickedness and the wickedness of their forefathers, in their unfaithfulness which they have committed against Me—and in their acting with hostility toward Me. Leviticus 26:40

In this next Scripture, Jesus carries sins from the Old Testament into the New Testament saying the people are guilty of sins that preceded them in past generations.

Fill up, then, the measure of your fathers' sins to the brim [so] that nothing may be wanting to a full measure]. You serpents! You spawn of vipers! How can you escape the penalty to be suffered in hell (Gehenna)? Because of this, take notice: I am sending you prophets and wise men (interpreters and teachers) and scribes (men learned in the Mosaic Law and the Prophets); some of them you will kill, even crucify, and some you will flog in your synagogues and pursue and persecute from town to town, So that upon your heads may come all the blood of the righteous shed on earth, from the blood of the righteous Abel to the blood of Zechariah son of Barachiah, whom you murdered between the sanctuary and the altar. Matthew 23:32-35

Jesus was admonishing the religious leaders, telling them that they would pay for their sins and the sins of their fathers. The NIV says, *Go ahead, then, and complete what your ancestors started!*

Further instructions

The first thing we do after we pray the repentance, renouncing, and forgiveness prayer, along with the breaking of curses over our lives, is to ask the person a few questions. We ask if they have any idea what demons they may have that need to go.

If they haven't thought of any or if the person hasn't had time to prepare in this way, we assure them that the Holy Spirit is faithful to expose the strongman and the demons under him to the person or to us.

Don't pray in the Spirit or claim the blood of Jesus

We instruct the person not to pray in the spirit or claim the blood of Jesus over themselves during their deliverance. To be clear, the person who receiving deliverance shouldn't be saying, "I am under the blood of Jesus" or "The blood of Jesus is against you" while they are in the process of getting their deliverance. This is because the demons would have to come out through the blood as they leave through the person's mouth, and they will fight that. We ask the person to just agree with us and command them to leave in the name of Jesus.

The Leader can say before they begin that "the Blood of Jesus is against you, so you will have to go." And they can say it at any time during the deliverance to encourage them to flee. We usually ask the Holy Spirit to shine His light from the bottom of the person's feet all the way up through their body to the top of their head and drive out all darkness.

Command demons to get into a basket

The Leader explains that they will be commanding the demons to get into a basket. The basket we use is a visual aid that can be very helpful to those receiving the deliverance. We ask the person to picture themselves holding a basket in their hands. They will be commanding the demons to get out of them and into the basket. After that, we instruct the person to give a good cough to get rid of any residue left by the demon.

After we complete each deliverance of the strongman and demons under him, we ask the person to hand the basket up to the Lord for Him to do what He wants with the demons and replace them with what is called a 'divine exchange.'

Quite often Jesus will put something as an exchange into the basket, and then we lower it back down. The person might either see something in the basket or the Holy Spirit will tell them what He is giving them in exchange. If they don't see or hear anything it's no problem. We quote the Word of what the scriptural exchange is for an infilling of the area that the strongman and the demons vacated to be well covered.

We find the reference for a basket of sin in Zechariah 5:6-8.

What is it?" I asked. He replied, "It is a basket for measuring grain, and it's filled with the sins of everyone throughout the land." Then the heavy lead cover was lifted off the basket, and there was a woman sitting inside it. The angel said, "The woman's name is Wickedness," and he pushed her back into the basket and closed the heavy lid again.

We can also reference the Scripture of casting our burdens onto the Lord.

*Cast your burden upon the LORD and He will sustain
you; He will never let the righteous be shaken.
Psalm 55:22 NIV*

As we command the strongman and his demons to get into the
basket, we are exchanging the yoke of demonic bondage for
the yoke of Divine blessings. Jesus reaffirms this in Matthew
11:29-30,

*Take My yoke upon you and learn from Me; for I am
gentle and humble in heart, and you will find rest for
your souls. For My yoke is easy and My burden is light."
(NKJV)*

More information before beginning the deliverance session

Jesus says in Mark 3:27,

*No man can enter into a strong man's house, and spoil
his goods, except he will first bind the strong man; and
then he will spoil his house. (KJV)*

It's logical to assume that when Jesus performed deliverance,
He would address the strongman in a person because that's
what the Word says to do. The following list contains the
names of strongmen that Jesus dealt with. The Word tells us
there are demons besides strongmen.

*And these signs will follow those who believe; In my
name they will cast out demons; they will speak in new
tongues. Mark 16:17 NKJV*

The list of names of the individual demons under each
strongman (found in Chapter 11) exhibit characteristics and
manifestations that point to their ruler, just as the symptoms
in a sick person point to a particular root of an illness. The
doctor doesn't medicate to cure symptoms but uses them to
help him heal the root cause if possible.

93

I know that some demons that I have named might be manifestations of the strongman they are listed under. But through our experience, we have also found some manifestations are demons, so we try the spirits as the Word says. If it's a manifestation then that is what it is, like a runny nose that comes with a cold. But if it is a demon, it will go if we command it.

Our objective is to bind and cast out the strongman and then command the demons who are manifesting under him to get out. The Holy Spirit will tell you if there are other demons we haven't listed that may be within you that need to go. It would be impossible to have a complete list. If other names of demons come to you as you are praying through each category, deal with them as you have the others.

Deliverance isn't a one-time thing. It's a work in progress. By that I mean as you live your life on this earth, it's possible and probable that you may unknowingly let demons come in. If a door is opened to them they could slip in. God is faithful if the person is staying on track with the Lord. He will reveal to you if you need deliverance, because once you have deliverance you will be alert.

Listed first are the strongmen and their definitions. Next are their characteristics and manifestations. Then the prayer for deliverance, which you can add to or change to suit your circumstances. The possible demons are listed under each strongman.

The last step is a decree of infilling of the Holy Spirit which will bring light into us. The Word that replaces the darkness is the divine exchange. I have taken the liberty to personalize the Scriptures when they work best as a decree. That won't offend the Father, in fact, He wants to make each Scripture personal and profitable to each of us.

All Scripture is God-breathed [given by divine inspiration] and is profitable for instruction, for conviction [of sin], for correction [of error and restoration to obedience], for training in righteousness [learning to live in conformity to God's will, both publicly and privately—behaving honorably with personal integrity and moral courage]; so that the man of God may be complete and proficient, outfitted and thoroughly equipped for every good work.
2 Timothy 3:16-17

Not everyone will relate to every strongman or demon listed under him. It doesn't hurt to pray about each one; no harm can come of it. You can't deliver a demon that isn't there, but there may be one hiding and you can get deliverance. There are always more strongmen than are listed. The Holy Spirit can reveal them to you, and you will be equipped to cast them out.

He is my refuge and my fortress, My God, in Him I will trust." Surely He shall deliver me from the snare of the fowler and from the perilous pestilence.

Psalm 91:2 NKJV

Chapter 11

Beginning the deliverance session

The leader begins the session with a prayer.

Thank You, Father God, that You give each of us, as your children, the power and authority to minister in Your name to release the captives and bring healing. We put on the full armor of God as Your Word says to do, which assures us of the victory over our unseen enemy.

We place the belt of truth around our waist, the breastplate of righteousness in place, our feet are fitted with the readiness that comes from the gospel of peace. We take up the shield of faith to extinguish all the flaming arrows of the evil one. We place the helmet of salvation over our minds and grasp the sword of the Spirit, which is the Word of God. (Ephesians 6:10-18)

Today is the day for deliverance and healing. We thank You for Your Holy Spirit who will bring the truth to light in our lives so we can see the lies that we have been believing and be set free from our burdens and bondages.

The leader continues with the Psalm 91 Scripture as a covering over everyone.

We declare Psalm 91 as protection over everyone present, our families, our friends, our jobs, our property, our finances, our health, our ministries, and anything else connected with us. In the name of Jesus.

He who dwells in the secret place of the Most High, shall abide under the shadow of the Almighty. We/I will say of the LORD, "He is my refuge and my fortress, My God, in Him I will trust." Surely He shall deliver me from the snare of the fowler and from the perilous pestilence.

He shall cover me with His feathers, and under His wings I shall take refuge; His truth shall be my shield and buckler. I shall not be afraid of the terror by night, nor of the arrow that flies by day, nor of the pestilence that walks in darkness, nor of the destruction that lays waste at noonday. A thousand may fall at my side, And ten thousand at my right hand; but it shall not come near me. Only with my eyes shall I look and see the reward of the wicked. Because I have made the LORD, who is my refuge, even the Most High, my dwelling place, no evil shall befall me, nor shall any plague come near my dwelling; for He shall give His angels charge over me, to keep me in all my ways. In their hands they shall bear me up, lest I dash my foot against a stone. I shall tread upon the lion and the cobra, the young lion, and the serpent I shall trample underfoot.

Because I have set my love upon You, therefore You will deliver me; You will set me on high, because I have known Your name. I shall call upon You, and You will answer me; You will be with me in trouble; You will deliver me and honor me. With long life You will satisfy me and show me Your salvation. Amen. (Psalm 91 NKJ)

Next, everyone prays this prayer together.

The leader can say the prayer and the person repeat it after the moderator, so it becomes a personal prayer for each person. When possible, have a printed copy to give each person so they can read along with everyone and then have it to take with them.

Dear Heavenly Father, I come before You today. I repent and renounce any sin or iniquity that I have committed against You or Your Word. I also stand in the gap repenting for any sin or iniquity that anyone in my generational bloodline may have committed against You or against Your Word.

As I pray my prayer of repentance, I include any ungodly oaths or vows spoken and agreed to by word or signature or any ungodly covenants made with secret societies such as Freemasonry, Shriners, Eastern Star, or any secret societies at different colleges and their fraternities. I repent and renounce and ask forgiveness for any occult witchcraft connections. I ask that any other secret societies that I am not aware of will be included in the list.

I repent on behalf of anyone in my generational bloodline, including myself, who has made a blood covenant with someone else in our ignorance, even as children. I repent for any broken marriage covenant vows through adultery or homosexuality or any other sexual perversion. If anyone in my generational bloodline has had or performed an abortion or murdered another person, or if I or anyone else have broken any of the Ten Commandments, I repent and renounce the sin and ask forgiveness.

I also forgive any person who has ever hurt or offended me. I release all unforgiveness, bitterness, or anger that I may have held against anyone. I send back anything that I may have received within my soulish carnal nature from any other person. I cut myself off from anything that I have received and anything that may still be affecting me in the soulish realm from any ungodly relationship. I release them and anything that is still attached from them to me, or from me to them completely.

I forgive anyone in my generational bloodline who has brought shame and curses upon me or others in my family *through their negative actions and lifestyle behaviors. I forgive myself as You have forgiven me.*

John 1:9 says, If we [freely] admit that we have sinned and confess our sins, He is faithful and just and will forgive our sins and cleanse us continually from all unrighteousness.

I thank You that all curses that have been operating using sin as their foundation or stronghold are now cut off from me and my generational bloodline, which includes the people above me who are still living and those below me.

Thank You, Lord, for Your grace and mercy as You forgive all recorded sins that are written in my Book of Life, as found in Psalm 139:16-18 which says: Your eyes have seen my unformed substance; And in Your book were written all the days that were appointed for me, when as yet there was not one of them [even taking shape].

I ask that as You extend forgiveness to my family bloodline, You will strike our sins and iniquities from each person's record book in heaven, replacing them with the cleansing testimony that we have in Jesus Christ that washes us clean before You. You paid the price for my freedom and my family's freedom totally, by shedding Your blood on the cross for each of our sins. Thank You Jesus, for Your blood sacrifice so I and my family can be set free and walk in liberty. I decree, as I apply the blood of Jesus to my generational bloodline, that we can have a DNA switch at the cellular level to wash all the sin and iniquity from our lineage and release healing.

I decree that all legal rights the accuser has been using against us in the spiritual realm have been erased as I have repented, renounced, and asked forgiveness for sin. All curses have been broken and all strongmen and the demons under them will have to go. They no longer have any legal right to operate in me and they no longer have any stronghold of a curse to hide within and attack me from.

The Bible says in Proverbs 26:2, As the bird by wandering, as a swallow by flying, so a curse without cause shall not alight.

I thank You that now I am empowered to resist the devil and He will flee from me.

James 4:7 says, "Resist the devil, and he will flee from you." And in John 10:10 it says, "The thief cometh not, but for to steal, and to kill, and to destroy. I have come that they might have life and that they might have it more abundantly."

Thank You, Lord, for Your great compassion and mercy upon me. Psalm 51:1 is my confession: Have mercy on me, O God, according to your unfailing love; according to your great compassion blot out my transgressions. Amen.

Because we have already covered all generational bloodline curses in our prayer before beginning deliverance you don't have to repeat it, so I won't include it in the deliverance prayers. The decree for the infilling will come at the end of the deliverance of each strongman and the demons under him have been evicted. Start with first strongman

1. Strongman of fear

Fear: to be afraid of something or someone: to expect or worry about something bad or unpleasant; to be afraid and worried.

Characteristics and manifestations: Demons under the spirit of fear: Fright, horror, fear of death, dread, terror, nightmares, anxiety, panic, worry, inferiority, fear of man, phobia, fear of darkness, heights, spirit of foreboding, spirit of shock and trauma.

For God did not give us a spirit of timidity or cowardice or fear, but [He has given us a spirit] of power and of love and of sound judgment and personal discipline [abilities that result in a calm, well-balanced mind, and self-control]. 2 Timothy 1:7

Fear is afraid that you will discover him and evict him. King David was no stranger to this spirit. He cries out to the Lord in Psalm 55:4-5.

My heart is in anguish within me, And the terrors of death have fallen upon me. Fear and trembling have come upon me; Horror has overwhelmed me.

In some situations a person can be frozen with fear. It is as if they are bound completely and cannot move, or in some cases, not even be able to speak out loud. This can happen especially at night lying in bed. The person is terrified.

Fear is the faith thief.

He said to them, "Why are you afraid, you men of little faith?" Then He got up and rebuked the winds and the sea, and there was [at once] a great and wonderful calm [a perfect peacefulness]. Matthew 8:26

The fear of man brings a snare. According to the Bible, fear will snare a person; it will trap them.

The fear of man brings a snare, But whoever trusts in and puts his confidence in the LORD will be exalted and safe. Proverbs 29:25

...that through death He might destroy him who had the power of death, that is, the devil, and release those who through fear of death were all their lifetime subject to bondage. Hebrews 2:14-15

Prayer for deliverance of the spirit of fear

Dear Jesus, I repent and renounce the strongman of fear. I ask You to forgive me for providing a home for this foul spirit and for believing him and thinking that I had to fear You, anything, or anyone in an unhealthy way. Thank You for forgiving me for allowing fear to rule within me.

I know that You love me, and You want me delivered of this spirit. I bind and command the spirit of fear to leave now, in the name of Jesus. You no longer have a home in me. You must go! You don't have a choice! Get into the basket now, in the name of Jesus. (Next, you can give a good cough or blow out forcefully to get rid of any residue left from it. If you can't see it, it's ok. Believe in faith that it has left you and gotten into the basket.) Then say, *Thank You, Jesus, for delivering me of the spirit of fear.*

(Next, one at a time, command each of the following demon spirits to get out of you and get in the basket. Give a good cough after each one.) *Fright, horror, fear of death, dread, terror, nightmares, anxiety, panic, worry, inferiority, fear of man, phobia, fear of darkness, heights, shock, and trauma leave me now!* (Give another good cough or blow out forcefully to get rid of any residue left from them.) *Thank You Jesus for delivering me.*

Holy Spirit as I wait on You, please reveal if there are any other spirits that need to go that I have missed that operate with these spirits.

If the Holy Spirit reveals any others, command them to get out and into the basket too. After the spirits all get into the basket, raise it up to the Lord. Wait for a minute to see or hear if He puts something special for Your divine exchange into it, then lower it back down and decree Your infilling.

Decree for infilling and divine exchange

I thank You that the only fear I will have is a healthy fear of Your name. I am in awe of who You are and how much You love me. I have nothing to fear. My past and my future is in Your hands. You love me and I trust You.

I decree and receive Proverbs 9:10, Instruct a wise man, and he will be wiser still; teach a righteous man, and he will increase his learning. The fear of the LORD is the beginning of wisdom, and knowledge of the Holy One is understanding. For through wisdom, my days will be multiplied, and years will be added to my life....

I sought the Lord and He answered me and delivered me from all my fears. (Psalm 34:4)

I thank You that I have been delivered of all fear, fright, horror, fear of death, dread, terror, nightmares, anxiety, panic, worry, inferiority, fear of man, phobia, fear of darkness, heights, and a spirit of foreboding.

I decree John 14:1: I will not let my heart be troubled. Thank You, Lord, for freeing me from all of these demons.

I believe what You say in John 4:18: There is no fear in love, but perfect love drives out fear.

I decree and fill myself with Your Word in Psalm 27: 1-2: The Lord is my light and my salvation—whom shall I fear? The Lord is the refuge and fortress of my life—whom shall I dread? I am now fearless for You, Lord!

2. Strongman of doubt and unbelief

Doubt: a feeling of uncertainty or lack of conviction.

Unbelief: lack of religious belief; an absence of faith, lack of trust.

Characteristics and manifestations: People can't rest in their faith and be at peace because they don't trust what the scriptures say. They always want proof because they have been robbed of their faith. They want to argue over miracles or signs and wonders. They can't comprehend them.

> So, we see that they were not able to enter [into His rest—the promised land] because of unbelief and an unwillingness to trust in God. Hebrews 3:19

Thomas, one of the disciples, needed proof that Jesus was who He said He was. They called him doubting Thomas.

> But Thomas, one of the twelve [disciples], who was called Didymus (the twin), was not with them when Jesus came. So, the other disciples kept telling him, "We have seen the Lord!" But he said to them, "Unless I see in His hands the marks of the nails, and put my finger into the nail prints, and put my hand into His side, I will never believe." Eight days later His disciples were again inside the house, and Thomas was with them. Jesus came, though the doors had been barred, and stood among them and said, "Peace to you." Then He said to Thomas, "Reach here with your finger, and see My hands; and put out your hand and place it in My side. Do not be unbelieving, but [stop doubting and] believe." Thomas answered Him, "My Lord and my God!" Jesus said to him, "Because you have seen Me, do you now believe? Blessed [happy, spiritually secure, and favored by God] are they who did not see [Me] and yet believed [in Me]." John 20:24-29

Fortunately, Jesus understands what a person is going through in their walk of faith and knows when it is a demonic stronghold that needs to be removed. He loves us and won't leave us the way we are. If a person sincerely wants to be closer to God and have a personal relationship with Jesus, all they need do is ask and Jesus will help them.

This demon will tell the person that because of their sins God will reject them and it will convince them to think their acceptance by God has to do with how good they are and what they can do to earn God's love.

Prayer for deliverance

I repent and renounce any sin that I have committed that allowed a spirit of doubt and unbelief to gain access to me. I ask You to forgive me for harboring that spirit. I thank You for Your forgiveness. I bind and command this strongman of doubt and unbelief to go now! You must leave me and get into the basket. (Now you can give a good cough or blow out forcefully to get rid of any residue left from it.)

Holy Spirit, as I wait on You, shine Your light from the bottom of my feet up through my body to the top of my head, driving out anything that is not of You. Reveal to me if there are any other spirits that need to leave me that operate with this doubt and unbelief.

When you have taken time to hear from the Lord, then lift the basket up to Him. Wait on the Holy Spirit to see if He wants to tell or show you anything. After waiting for a minute or so lower it back down to receive the gift of the infilling.

Decree for infilling and divine exchange

Now that the strongman spirit of doubt and unbelief has left me, I decree my infilling of the Holy Spirit. I receive the divine exchange within me. I fill that space with Godly peace, and I will be able to rest and build trust and spiritual strength. I will believe Your whole Word, and nothing will be impossible for me!

Matthew 17:19 tells me if I have faith the size of a mustard seed, I will say to this mountain, 'Move from here to there,' and it will move, and nothing will be impossible for me.

I fill myself with faith and I decree Proverbs 3:5–8; I will trust in the Lord with all my heart and lean not on my own understanding; in all my ways I will submit to him, and he will make my paths straight. I will not be wise in my own eyes; I will fear the Lord and shun evil. This will bring health to my body and nourishment to my bones.

I thank You, Lord, for my new life of freedom. Holy Spirit, as I wait on You, please reveal if there are any other spirits that need to go that I have missed that operate with this spirit of doubt and unbelief. Amen. (If any more come to your mind repeat the procedure for getting rid of them.)

3. Strongman of rejection

Rejection: the act of not accepting, believing, or considering something: the state of being rejected; negativity.

> *Whoever listens to you listens to me; whoever rejects you rejects me, but whoever rejects me rejects him who sent me." Luke 10:16*

Characteristics and manifestations: Rejection is something that none of us can escape while we live here on earth. Sooner or later, we will each have at least one opportunity to deal with rejection. It is a painful experience that some handle better than others. Of course, it depends on who has rejected you and how close they are to you, and your emotional state. Rejection opens the doors to many more evil spirits that move in with it.

Those that can truly forgive others, themselves, and sometimes God, are able to move on in their lives and don't usually have to deal with the spirit of rejection. But for those who aren't in a good place when rejection happens to them and are unable to handle it in a healthy spiritual way, they open a door into their lives that the spirit of rejection comes through and makes itself at home.

The person doesn't usually realize what is happening to them in the spiritual realm concerning opening that door, but it will affect them in the physical realm. It is natural for our soul nature to embrace the offense and begin to justify our feelings of offense in many ways.

There is another way this spirit can enter a person and that is through the womb of a mother, if the baby she is carrying is unwanted or through a botched abortion. As the baby grows the child may struggle with a seemingly unfounded spirit of feeling unloved, much like an orphan; even if the child was put up for adoption and has been adopted by loving parents. The child may struggle with a feeling of inferiority and not understand why. They may not recognize they suffer from this, but often others can see it in them.

Other root causes could be physical or sexual abuse of the mother when the baby was in the womb, or after their birth, as babies or very young children.

Emotional trauma from being rejected by others throughout a person's life opens doors of darkness. If a person is a completely innocent party to what has occurred in their life, it won't stop a spirit who is looking for any opportunity to enter a person to come into them. Anger and offense work alongside this strongman.

The spirit of rejection doesn't care about the person it manages to get into. It is out to destroy them and take them over so it can run their lives. This demonic spirit tells a person in their mind that they are unlovable for who they are, and they don't measure up because they are undeserving of anyone's love. This breeds resentment and bitterness. Rejection will demand that a person reject themselves as being worthy of the Lord.

One of the ways it may manifest is through a mindset that says a person has to be perfect and have everything around them perfect to be accepted and loved. It will compel them to set standards too high for themselves and sometimes others that are close to them. This could include spouses or children that they end up rejecting and getting rejected by because of this spirit. Because they don't know how to love themselves, they are unable to love others or receive love from others in a healthy way.

Rejection leaves a trail all around the person. The person is blinded and usually can't see why others reject them. They blame everything on everyone else, at their work or in their families.

One way to tell if you are dealing with this demon would be to look at your life. Have you had to deal with a lot of rejection? Maybe it's not others, but what is going on within you.

Prayer for deliverance

Dear Heavenly Father, I repent for believing what this foul spirit has said about me instead of believing what you say about me. I ask forgiveness for any sin that has allowed this spirit of rejection to enter me. I bind, rebuke, and renounce this spirit of rejection and I command you to leave me now. Be gone. You no longer have a home. I reject you completely. Get into the basket now.

1 John 1:9 says that as I confess my sins, he is faithful and just to forgive me of my sins and to cleanse me from all unrighteousness.

(Next, you can give a good cough or blow out forcefully to get rid of any residue left by the spirit of rejection.)

Thank You, Jesus, for this word which is a death blow to any demonic spirit within me. Your Word says that You will cleanse me and set me free.

a. Demon of unforgiveness

Unforgiveness: unwilling or unable to forgive. Having or making no allowance for error or weakness.

Some of the last words that Jesus spoke before He died concerned unforgiveness.

> *Then Jesus said, "Father, forgive them, for they do not know what they are doing." Luke 23:34*

Characteristics and manifestations: The spirit will not allow forgiveness. A person suffering under this spirit might say they forgive but feelings of offense keep cropping up driving a wedge that proves otherwise. If a person can't forgive, the demon spirit will keep bringing the offense up in their mind, so they are never at peace. It will wear a person down emotionally. This spirit will tell them they are a terrible person because they can't forgive then, on the other hand, it won't allow it.

> *Jesus said, "For if ye forgive men their trespasses, your heavenly Father will also forgive you: but if ye forgive not men their trespasses, neither will your Father forgive your trespasses. Matthew 6:14–15 NKJV*

Jesus instructed His disciples to forgive in Matthew 18:21–22.

> *Then Peter came to Jesus and asked, "Lord, how many times shall I forgive my brother or sister who sins against me? Up to seven times?" Jesus answered, "I tell you, not seven times, but seventy-seven times.*

He was clear that they were to live a lifestyle of forgiveness that offered freedom from the consequences of unforgiveness and bitterness.

Prayer for deliverance

Dear Heavenly Father, I repent and renounce the sin of unforgiveness. I ask You to forgive me for harboring unforgiveness. I completely forgive anyone who has wronged me. (You may need to name them) *I release every memory that I used to hold on to that allowed a spirit of unforgiveness to enter me.*

Spirit of unforgiveness, get out of me now. You no longer have a home. You have been discovered and I don't want anything to do with you. I command you to climb into the basket now. You don't have a choice. I, and the name of Jesus, are against you.

(Now you can give a good cough or blow out forcefully to get rid of any residue.)

Then decree: *Thank You Jesus for delivering me of the spirit of unforgiveness.*

b. Demon spirit of offense

Offense: The act of causing anger, resentment, displeasure, or affront. The state of being offended.

Characteristics and manifestations: The job of the spirit of offense is to break up unity between people and cause division in every area of a person's life.

> *Judge not, and you will not be judged; condemn not, and you will not be condemned; forgive, and you will be forgiven. Luke 6:37*

A brother offended is harder to be won than a strong city: and their contentions are like the bars of a castle. Proverbs 18:19

In their anger and hurt, a person might put up walls or a "fence" because of an offense. A person may believe it is wise to protect themselves from further hurt. These walls that a person might think are walls of protection become bars of bondage, and a person offended puts themselves in a self-created prison cell. That's the goal of this demon.

A person's wisdom yields patience; it is to one's glory to overlook an offense. Proverbs 19:11

A fool's anger is known at once, but a prudent man overlooks an insult. Proverbs 12: 16

Prayer for deliverance

Dear Jesus, I repent and renounce a spirit of offense. I ask You to forgive me for offending anyone and for being offended by anyone at any time in my life up to now, which includes being offended by family members. I forgive anyone who has ever offended me.

I repent and ask forgiveness if I have ever been offended at You. Maybe You didn't answer my prayers the way I thought You should, or things occurred in my life, and I got angry at You. Thank You for forgiving me. I know that You love me, and You want me delivered of this spirit.

In Jesus' name, I command the spirit of offense to get out! You no longer have a home. I have discovered you and I command you to get in the basket and do it now. You don't have a choice because I speak to you with the authority of Jesus Christ.

Spirit of judgment you must leave now too, in the name of Jesus. I repent for judgments I have made against others in

my anger and hurt. Get in the basket now, in Jesus' name.
(Now you can give a good cough or blow out forcefully to get rid of any residue from the spirits.)

Thank You Jesus for delivering me of the spirit of offense and judgment.

c. Demon spirit of anger

Anger: a strong feeling of displeasure and usually of antagonism. a threatening or violent appearance or state: rage

> *Refrain from anger and forsake wrath! Fret not yourself; it tends only to evil. Proverbs 37:8.*

> *Whoever is slow to anger has great understanding, but he who has a hasty temper exalts folly. Proverbs 14:29*

Characteristics and manifestations: Anger is usually right out in the open. It is hard to hide. A person who struggles with unresolved anger and wrath will demonstrate a variety of behaviors that indicate his inner battle. Even though an angry person might deny having a "problem" with anger, those closest to him or her—spouse, children, and coworkers—will attest to seeing the evidence of anger in his or her behavior.

Anger causes a person to become irritated with situations and circumstances that would not bother him otherwise. Anger affects the facial features and empowers a penetrating glare, pronounced frown, furrowed brows, tense facial muscles, flushed complexion, prominent veins, and enlarged pupils.

Prayer for deliverance for the spirit of anger
Dear Heavenly Father, I thank You that You have revealed to me that I have this spirit of anger and it is preventing me from living a peaceful life. I repent for harboring the spirit of anger. I ask forgiveness for my actions, and I renounce the

spirit of anger. I command you, spirit of anger, to leave me now, in the name of Jesus. I refuse to allow you to influence me anymore. Get out, in Jesus' name. You no longer have a home and must leave now. Climb into the basket now in Jesus' name!

(Next, you can give a good cough or blow out forcefully to get rid of it.)

Thank You, Jesus, for delivering me of the spirit of anger.

d. Demon of an orphan spirit

Orphan: An orphan is a child whose parents have died, are unknown or have permanently abandoned them.

Characteristics and manifestations: Because of the spirit of rejection, a person might be dealing with an orphan spirit, especially if the person was given up by their parents for adoption. Jesus says in His Word that He has adopted us. Jesus was the adopted child of Joseph. No person who is saved is an orphan or a foster child of God. There are no foster children in the Bible. We have been adopted by Jesus and we have become true sons and daughters of Christ.

Foster children have no legal right to any inheritance from those raising them, but adopted children have every legal right for inheritance that a natural child has. I add this about foster children because a lady once told me that she had always been told that Jesus was a foster child of Joseph.

Jesus completely understands what a person who was an orphan or who was adopted may be going through, because He went through it with people who knew He wasn't Joseph's child. I am sure that some were mean and said things to try to hurt Him with rejection.

Romans 8:15 says,

For I have not received the spirit of bondage again to fear; but I have received the Spirit of adoption, whereby I cry, 'Abba! Father!'

Galatians 4:6 says,

And because you are sons, God has sent the Spirit of His Son into our hearts, crying, Abba! Father!

Prayer for deliverance

I repent and renounce an orphan spirit. I ask forgiveness for harboring this spirit. I am not an orphan and I command you orphan spirit to leave me, in Jesus' name! You no longer have a home or any authority to operate within me. I reject you completely. I have a full inheritance through Jesus Christ. I am adopted into the family of God. Get out of me in the name of Jesus and climb into the basket now. (Next, you can give a good cough or blow out forcefully to get rid of any residue that may have left behind.)

e. Demon spirit of resentment and bitterness

Bitterness: Harboring bitterness and resentment in your heart brings consequences that affect you physically, mentally, emotionally, and spiritually.

The spirit of offense works best with rejection. When a person gets insulted, they usually get angry or hurt and reject the person who offends them. The goal of the demon is to move the person further into sin by getting them to begin to judge the person who hurt them. Once the accuser can get us to side with him by judging, the Lord has to judge us.

Beloved, never avenge yourselves, but leave it to the wrath of God, for it is written, "Vengeance is mine, I will repay, says the Lord." Romans 12:19

Characteristics and manifestations: It has been proven that bitterness and resentment weaken the immune system, which can lead to physical ailments. It requires emotional energy to maintain a grudge. Undealt with, resentment and bitterness can grow to cause you to hate someone. This causes the body to produce hormones to cope with the stress which will lead to chronic fatigue and adrenal exhaustion, among other things. Bitterness pollutes the whole body. This will cause a person to not be able to handle everyday things that pop up and cause them more stress. A person could become so emotionally focused on the person who offended them that they lose focus on their life and responsibilities. These emotions will affect their relationship with God. He has a lot to say in the Bible about this topic.

For I see that you are full of bitterness and captive to sin." Acts 8:23

See to it that no one falls short of the grace of God and that no bitter root grows up to cause trouble and defile many. Hebrews 12:15

Grieve not the Holy Spirit of God, whereby ye are sealed unto the day of redemption. Let all bitterness, and wrath, and anger, and clamor, and evil speaking, be put away from you, with all malice: and be ye kind one to another, tenderhearted, forgiving one another, even as God for Christ's sake hath forgiven you.
Ephesians 4:30–32

Prayer for deliverance

Dear Heavenly Father, I repent, renounce, and ask forgiveness for harboring a spirit of bitterness and resentment. I completely forgive anyone who has mistreated me in any way. I release all resentment and bitterness that I have held against anyone who has hurt me. (You may need to name them). I thank You that I can cast out the spirit of resentment and bitterness by the power of Your name. Spirit of resentment and bitterness, get out now! You no longer have a home. You have been discovered and I don't want anything to do with you. I command you to climb into the basket now. You don't have a choice. Jesus and I are against you.

Thank You Jesus for delivering me of the spirit of resentment and unforgiveness. (Now you can give a good cough or blow out forcefully to get rid of any residue.)

Decree for infilling and divine exchange for the strongman of rejection. orphan spirit, spirit of resentment, judgment, and bitterness, the spirit of offense, anger, and unforgiveness.

I thank You, Jesus, that as I read Your Word, I understand that You were rejected also. You know exactly how I feel, and You are my example of how to handle rejection.

Isaiah 53:3 says, He was despised and rejected by men, A Man of sorrows and pain and acquainted with grief; And like One from whom men hide their faces. He was despised, and we did not appreciate His worth or esteem Him.

Jesus, I want You to know that I appreciate and worship You, and I receive complete deliverance from the spirit of rejection. I embrace Your divine exchange of infilling of Your love and healing. I say Abba Father to You – My Father!

I decree over myself what Jesus said in John 6:37: "However, those the Father has given me will come to Me, and I will never reject them," and Psalm 27:10 that says; "Even if my father and mother abandon me, the Lord will hold me close" I receive the divine exchange of the spirit of adoption in place of the orphan right now.

Thank You, Lord, for Your perfect love that You freely give to me. I accept it in every area of my life. My life was not a mistak but was planned in your book about me in heaven, no matter what circumstances were happening when I was conceived and in the womb. I will fill the vacant space that the orphan spirit left with adoption, acceptance, and love.

I fill every place that the spirit of resentment left within me when it left, with peace and contentment in every area of my life. I fill every area the spirit of judgment left with faith and trust in You, Jesus. I am not the judge. You are and I am content to let You be the Judge.

I fill every area that bitterness, offense, anger, and unforgiveness have left within me as they left with Your perfect peace and unity.

I decree Psalm 133 over myself: Behold, how good and how pleasant it is for brethren to dwell together in unity! It is like the precious ointment upon the head, that ran down upon the beard, even Aaron's beard: that went down to the skirts of his garments; As the dew of Hermon, and as the dew that descended upon the mountains of Zion: for there the Lord commanded the blessing, even life forevermore.

I thank You that Your Word and Your presence will fill my heart and calm my nerves whenever anger attempts to get me to open a door for it to come back in. I decree that I will follow the example Jesus set when He had every opportunity to be angry but was able to calmly deal with antagonistic people in different situations.

You are within me, and You give me peace that is beyond my understanding. I refuse frustration. I will follow Your Word which says in Ephesians 4:26-27, "Be angry and do not sin: do not let the sun go down on your wrath, nor give place to the devil."

I will give him no place. I thank You for replacing all unforgiveness, resentment, and bitterness with Your peace

*and Your joy. I thank You for a new anointing to fill me and
release the gifts of Your spirit which are wisdom,
understanding, counsel, fortitude, knowledge, piety, and fear
of the Lord within me.*

4. Strongman of bondage

Bondage: slave, a state of being bound usually by compulsion
(as of law or mastery): such as captivity, serfdom b: servitude
or subjugation to a controlling person or force. young people
in bondage to drugs or other addictions.

> *For freedom, Christ has set us free; stand firm
> therefore, and do not submit again to a yoke of slavery.
> Galatians 5:1*

Characteristics and manifestations: Unable to apply self-
control to impulses that a person knows are negative and
damaging to their lives. To feel driven to do something. The
enemy drives a person. The Holy Spirit leads a person.

A person with an addiction will feel a strong compulsion to act
on their feelings or a demand of the body. Some examples are
out of control eating, gambling, smoking, drinking, inability to
break free from habits that put a person in bondage to sin of
any kind.

> *For all that is in the world—the lust and sensual craving
> of the flesh and the lust and longing of the eyes and the
> boastful pride of life [pretentious confidence in one's
> resources or in the stability of earthly things]—these do
> not come from the father but are from the world.
> 1 John 2:16*

Prayer for deliverance

*Lord, I repent and renounce any sin that I have committed in
my life that has opened a door and allowed a spirit of
bondage to place me in slavery to it. I repent for my actions*

and how I have hurt others due to every addiction that I struggle with. I ask Your forgiveness for that sin against my body and for allowing a strongman to work within me to keep me in bondage.

I acknowledge that addictions have become idols in my life. I repent for promoting spiritual growth for the kingdom of darkness within myself and I ask forgiveness for that. As I have asked for forgiveness and received it from You, I break every curse that has allowed a spirit of bondage to torment me.

I bind and command the spirit of bondage to leave me now in the name of Jesus. You no longer have a home in me. Get into the basket right now in the name of Jesus.

I command any demon of addiction, drugs, alcohol, cigarettes, food, gambling, pornography, or lust to leave me. Get out of me all of you and get into the basket now.

I remind you of the repentance prayer for my generational bloodline that gives me every legal right to cut my generational bloodline off from all curses to do with bondages in the name of Jesus and set everyone free who has struggled with these demons in my family due to the curse of generational sin to be set free.

Command each addiction or bondage by name to get into the basket then say, "*Thank You Jesus for delivering me of the spirit of _____.* (Raise the basket up to the Lord and give it to Him.)

Holy Spirit, as I wait on You, please reveal if there are any other spirits that I may have missed that operate with this spirit of bondage and need to go.

Decree for infilling and divine exchange
I decree an infilling of Your Word within me as a divine exchange in my life. For freedom, Christ has set me free; I

will stand firm, therefore, and will not submit again to a yoke of slavery. (Galatians 5:1)

I decree Philippians 4:13, I can do all things through Him who strengthens and empowers me. I am self-sufficient in Christ's sufficiency; thank You for my divine exchange. You are infusing me with inner strength through the Holy Spirit who is my encourager and comforter. Thank You, Lord, that You are faithful and will establish me and guard me against the evil one according to Your Word.

But now that I have been set free from sin and have become a slave to God, the new fruit I will produce and reap in my new life will lead to holiness, and my assured outcome is eternal life. (Romans 6:22) Amen.

5. Strongman of heaviness/grief

Heaviness: a load, typically a heavy one. Heavy burden. A duty or misfortune that causes hardship, anxiety, or grief. A nuisance.

Characteristics and manifestations: Excessive mourning, sorrow, grief, insomnia, self-pity, broken-heart, despair, dejection, hopelessness, depression, suicidal thoughts, inner hurts, heaviness

Extended grief can be a manifestation of heaviness. Sometimes when a person loses a loved one, they can find themselves stuck in heavy grief even years later after the death. They may not realize they are stuck, and it could be a spirit that saw an opportunity to enter when they were going through the season of grief because of the loss of a loved one, or any other traumatic experience in their life that was a major loss to them.

Reproach hath broken my heart, and I am full of heaviness: and I looked for some to take pity, but there

was none, and for comforters, but I found none.
Psalm 69:20

In 1969, Elisabeth Kübler-Ross, a Swiss-American psychiatrist introduced a model regarding the '5 Stages of Grief' in a book called *On Death and Dying*. This grief model was one of the first models used to help individuals recognize the stages of grief and the effect it can cause. In the original book, Elisabeth Kübler-Ross referenced five stages of grief: denial, anger, bargaining, depression, and acceptance.

Through time, however, different sources have added what they believe to be other stages of grief. While grief models are often used to help individuals who are grieving understand the process and how to move forward, not everyone experiences the same order of grief stages or even experiences every stage.

Testimony: My sister and I were once delivered of a spirit of heaviness/grief that saw an opportunity and jumped on both of us. We weren't the ones suffering the loss of a loved one, but our empathy for those who were going through the loss saw an opportunity and took it.

We were driving to a prayer meeting and had stopped at a red light. Going through the light in the opposite direction was a long line of cars in a funeral procession. We began to pray for the people in genuine sincerity for their loss. Suddenly we both began to cry. Tears poured down our faces and we couldn't stop them. We looked at each other in shock.

We were only about five minutes from the home where we were going to the meeting. When we got there and went up to the door and knocked, we both still had tears running down our faces. We couldn't figure out what was happening to us. We each felt a real depressive heaviness upon us. When the woman who was conducting the prayer meeting answered the door she said, "Oh my! What has happened?" We explained what had happened, and she said, "Oh, you have had a spirit of grief attack you." At that, she commanded the spirit of grief to leave us in Jesus' name. That spirit lifted off both of us and it was gone for good. That was an amazing testimony to us about how a spirit can attack a person.

A heart full of joy and goodness makes a cheerful face, but when a heart is full of sadness the spirit is crushed. Proverb 15:13

David described what extended grief will do to a person.

Be gracious to me, O Lord, for I am in distress; my eye is wasted from grief; my soul and my body also. For my life is spent with sorrow, and my years with sighing; my strength fails because of my iniquity, and my bones waste away. Psalm 31: 9-10

It's difficult for a person who stays in grief to be comforted, but when they move into mourning, they can be comforted.

Blessed are those who mourn, for they shall be comforted. Matthew5:4

That is not to say a person should try to follow the steps in the grieving process of the loss of a loved one, because everyone processes loss differently. But be aware that a spirit could attach to any of these steps, without the person realizing it. If a person just can't seem to move on after the death of a loved one and find themselves crying all the time for a long period of time, meaning years, it could be a spirit that took advantage of an opportunity.

But we do not want you to be uninformed, brothers, about those who are asleep, that you may not grieve as others do who have no hope. 1 Thessalonians 4:13

The Scripture says Jesus bore our grief.

*Surely, He has borne our griefs and carried our grief;
yet we esteemed Him stricken, smitten by God, and
afflicted.   Isaiah 53:4*

We all go through different seasons in our lives, but it helps us to understand that we might be stuck and not be able to move on because of a demon. And sometimes what we think is grief may actually be loneliness. It isn't a deliverance issue, you may need to take other steps to alleviate the real issue, such as counseling.

*For everything, there is a season, and a time for every
matter under heaven: a time to be born, and a time to
die; a time to plant, and a time to pluck up what is
planted; a time to kill, and a time to heal; a time to
break down, and a time to build up; a time to weep,
and a time to laugh; a time to mourn, and a time to
dance; a time to cast away stones, and a time to gather
stones together; a time to embrace, and a time to
refrain from embracing;   Ecclesiastes 3:1-14*

Prayer for deliverance

*Dear Jesus, I repent and renounce the strongman of
heaviness and grief. I ask You to forgive me for providing a
home for this foul spirit and for thinking that I had to carry
this heaviness by believing the lies that it has told me. I bind
you, spirit of heaviness and grief, and command you to get
out of me and climb into the basket. Leave me now, in the
name of Jesus! You don't have a choice, get out!* (Next, you
can give a good cough or blow out forcefully.)

Thank You Jesus for delivering me of the spirit of heaviness.

Next, command each spirit individually to get out and get into the basket: The spirit of mourning, sorrow, grief, insomnia, self-pity, broken-heart, despair, dejection, hopelessness, depression, suicidal thoughts, inner hurts, heaviness

Holy Spirit, as I wait on You, please reveal if there are any other spirits that I have missed that operate with this strongman of heaviness and grief and that need to go.

When you are comfortable that you have cast out every one of the demons, raise the basket up to the Lord. Wait a few minutes to see if He puts anything into the basket or says anything, then lower and decree Your divine exchange.

Decree for infilling and divine exchange

Thank You, Jesus, for delivering me from all heaviness and grief and from every demon that was operating under their command within me.

I believe and confess that Psalm 34:17-18 is for me: When the righteous cry, the Lord hears and rescues them from all their distress and troubles. The Lord is near to the heartbroken and He saves those who are crushed in spirit. Thank You for filling me with Your Word which brings Your light to me.

I thank You, Jesus, for setting me free from the spirit of heaviness and grief. I receive the garment of praise spoken of in Isaiah 61:3, To appoint unto them that mourn in Zion, to give unto them beauty for ashes, the oil of joy for mourning, the garment of praise for the spirit of heaviness; that they might be called trees of righteousness, the planting of the Lord, that He might be glorified. I thank You for my divine exchange.

I decree Luke 4:18 over myself: The Spirit of the Lord is on me because He has anointed me to proclaim good news to the poor. He has sent me to proclaim freedom for the prisoners and recovery of sight for the blind, to set the oppressed free.

6. Strongman of Infirmity

Infirmity: The quality or state of being infirm. the condition of being feeble: frailty, disease, malady.

Characteristics and manifestations: bent body-spine, impotent, frail, lame, asthma, Hay Fever, allergies, arthritis, weakness, lingering disorders, oppression, cancer

> *And there was a woman who for eighteen years had had an illness caused by a spirit (demon). She was bent double and could not straighten up at all. When Jesus saw her, He called her over and said to her, "Woman, you are released from your illness." Then He laid His hands on her, and immediately she stood erect again and she began glorifying and praising God.*
> *Luke 13:11-13*

Prayer for deliverance

Dear Jesus, I repent for any sin that has allowed a spirit of infirmity to live in me. I renounce the spirit of infirmity. I ask You to forgive me for committing any sin that opened a door for this foul spirit to inhabit me. I acknowledge that I have also repented for any sin that it could be operating under that came from my generational bloodline. The charge that the accuser has been using against me has been removed from the books in heaven.

Any curse that the demon of infirmity was functioning under has been removed. All legal rights for it to operate in me or the generations under me are washed away by the blood of Jesus. I bind the spirit of infirmity and command you to get out of me and climb into the basket. Leave now in the name of Jesus. You have been discovered and no longer have a home. You are not welcome here. You don't have a choice now go!

126

I ask You to quicken me anytime I am about to call any illness or infirmity mine, such as "my sugar diabetes, my arthritis, my headaches" I will never acknowledge the ownership of them or any other illness again. I cancel every diagnosis of any of these infirmities such as Bent Body-Spine (scoliosis), Impotent, Frail, Lame, Asthma-Hay Fever-Allergies, Arthritis, Weakness, Lingering Disorders, Oppression, Cancer, spoken over me by any doctor.

I command the spirit of infirmity to get out of me and into the basket. I also command each spirit as I name it to get into the basket. Scoliosis or any other bone disease, any Impotent-Frail-Lame, Asthma-Hay Fever-Allergies, Arthritis, Weakness, Lingering Disorders, Oppression, Cancer leave me now and get into the basket.

Holy Spirit, as I wait on You, please reveal if there are any other spirits that need to go that I have missed that operate with this spirit of infirmity. I raise this basket full of these demons and give it to You. (Wait a minute to see if you see or hear anything from the Holy Spirit, then lower it back down.)

Prayer for infilling

Dear Jesus, Thank You for delivering me from the curse of this foul spirit. I receive Your divine exchange of healing, strength, and energy within every cell of my body. I speak to every organ, cell, bones, skin, eyes, ears, muscles, veins, arteries, and every other part of my body that this and any other spirit related to it have negatively affected. In the name of Jesus, I speak renewal, restoration, and healing. I receive the divine exchange of these things and decree the cleansing blood of Jesus is flowing through my body purifying and energizing me, washing away everything that is not of Him.

Holy Spirit, shine Your light into any dark places of my inner man and illuminate Yourself through me, for Your glory. I decree Jeremiah 17:14 and declare, Heal me, O Lord, and I

127

will be healed; save me and I will be saved, for You are the one I praise."

I claim Acts 7:37-38. You know what has happened throughout the province of Judea, beginning in Galilee after the baptism that John preached. How God anointed Jesus of Nazareth with the Holy Spirit and power, and how He went around doing good and healing all who were under the power of the devil because God was with Him.

Thank You that You are alive today and performing miracles of healing on all those who ask. Amen.

7. Strongman of a deaf and dumb spirit

This is the definition of a deaf and dumb spirit from the Bible. Scriptures that describe this demon.

A man in the crowd answered, "Teacher, I brought You my son, who is possessed by a spirit that has robbed him of speech. Whenever it seizes him, it throws him to the ground. He foams at the mouth, gnashes his teeth, and becomes rigid. I asked Your disciples to drive out the spirit, but they could not." When Jesus saw that a crowd was running to the scene, He rebuked the impure spirit. "You deaf and mute spirit," He said, "I command you, come out of him and never enter him again."
Mark 9:17-18

Characteristics and manifestations: The scripture above gives physical manifestations of the spirit. It seems that this is one spirit. This tells us that this spirit manifests in seizures and it tries to kill a person or torment them terribly. This strongman can be delivered, but as Jesus says it will require prayer and fasting.

The Bible speaks of those who may not manifest this spirit in the same physical way, with seizures, but are spiritually asleep. They hear but don't hear. They see but don't really perceive what they are seeing, which is a form of spiritual slumber. This slumber spirit works together with the deaf and dumb spirit to lull people into submission so it can perform its will for them.

> *According as it is written, God hath given them the spirit of slumber, eyes that they should not see, and ears that they should not hear unto this day." Romans 11:8 KJV*

This is due to rebellious people who refused to hear the truth and to see the truth when it was before their eyes—Jesus performing miracles of healing and deliverance. Their rebellion against God caused Him to judge them.

> *You stiff-necked and stubborn people, uncircumcised in heart and ears, you are always actively resisting the Holy Spirit. You are doing just as your fathers did. Acts 7:51*
>
> *...for the Lord has poured over you a spirit of deep sleep. He has closed your eyes, [you who are] the prophets; and He has covered your heads, [you who are] the seers. Isaiah 29:10*
>
> *Go to this people and say, "You will be ever hearing but never understanding; you will be ever seeing but never perceiving." For this people's heart has become calloused; they hardly hear with their ears, and they have closed their eyes. Otherwise, they might see with their eyes, hear with their ears, understand with their hearts and turn, and I would heal them. Acts 28:26-27.*

Prayer for deliverance

Dear Jesus, I repent and ask forgiveness for any sin that allowed this deaf and dumb spirit to come upon me and operate within me. I ask forgiveness for all sin. I renounce any deaf and dumb spirit that gained a legal right to enter me because of my sin of refusing to see or hear. I bind it and

129

command it to leave me now, in Jesus' name. I thank You, Jesus, for revealing this to me.

I repent for the times in my life that You have spoken to me and I have not listened to You. I am guilty of ignoring words spoken by the Holy Spirit to me. I repent and ask forgiveness for the times You have tried to show me the truth in situations that I needed help with, and I refused to see what You were showing me because I thought my way was better. I silenced You and the Holy Spirit

I command the strongman of the deaf and dumb spirit to climb into the basket now. I also command a spirit of slumber that works with the deaf and dumb spirit to get out now! You must leave; you don't have a choice. Climb into the basket now.

2 Corinthians 3:14-16 holds a promise for me. It says that even though the veil is over my eyes due to this spirit, it will be taken away when I repent and turn to seek the Lord and the Holy Spirit. The Word says I will be transformed.

But their minds were made dull, for to this day the same veil remains when the old covenant is read. It has not been removed, because only in Christ is it taken away. Even to this day when Moses is read, a veil covers their hearts. But whenever anyone turns to the Lord, the veil is taken away. Now the Lord is the Spirit, and where the Spirit of the Lord is, there is freedom. And we all, who with unveiled faces contemplate the Lord's glory, are being transformed into his image with ever-increasing glory, which comes from the Lord, who is the Spirit.

I apply the redemption in this Word to myself. I see the truth and it has set me free and I am being transformed. (Next, give a good cough or blow out forcefully to get rid of any residue left from any of them)

Thank You Jesus for delivering me of the strongman of deaf and dumb spirit and thank You for removing any spirit of slumber.

a. Demon spirit of suicide

The definition of this demon is self-explanatory. I am putting it under the deaf and dumb strongman because we see in Scripture that this spirit would throw the boy into the fire and into the water to either burn him to death or drown him.

Characteristics and manifestations: A person has impulses to commit suicide. They think about death a lot and have an unnatural interest in death and suicide. They are drawn to movies and stories about the kingdom of darkness, subjects of suicide and death. Demons of depression, sadness, hopelessness, and self-pity all work together and need to be cast out individually.

Prayer for deliverance

I repent and ask forgiveness for my actions which have invited a spirit of death to gain access to my mind, will, and emotions. I bind all demons and evil spirits that are causing me to feel depressed and suicidal, in Jesus' name!

I command each one of you to get out of me in Jesus' name. I command suicide to go now! Climb in the basket. I command death to go now! Climb in the basket. I command depression to go now! Climb into the basket. Sadness—go now! Climb into the basket. Hopelessness—go now! Climb into the basket. Self-pity—go now! Climb into the basket!

None of you have any choice in this. I break every curse that has been working against me to bring these evil intentions of the enemy to fulfillment in my life. I cancel every demonic assignment concerning this subject against me and anyone my family, in Jesus' name. (Next, give a good cough or blow out forcefully to get rid of any residue left behind by them.)

Thank You, Jesus, for delivering me of these spirits of death, suicide, and everyone with them.

Holy Spirit, as I wait on You, please reveal if there are any other spirits that I have missed that operate with this deaf and dumb spirit and the spirit of slumber and need to go. (Wait a bit to see if the Holy Spirit does or says anything, then raise the basket up to Him. Wait a minute to see if He puts anything into the basket for you. Then you can lower it back down. Even if you see Him put something in the basket for you as a divine exchange, decree the divine exchange with your mouth to make sure you have completely filled the vacant space the demons have left.)

Decree for infilling and divine exchange

Dear Jesus, Thank You for delivering me from the spirit of death. I decree that I will receive the divine exchange of the promise in 2 Corinthians 3:16: Even to this day when Moses is read, a veil covers their hearts. But whenever anyone turns to the Lord, the veil is taken away.

To repent is to turn. As I have repented and asked forgiveness for my sins, the Lord will give me the divine exchange. Thank You, Lord, for Your faithfulness to remove the veil off the eyes of my understanding and that I will be able to see what You want me to see.

I activate my will to perform Your will. I am no longer asleep. I am awake and ready for action. I will be as Saul/Paul was when the veils came off his eyes in Acts 9:18. At that instant, something like scales fell from Saul's eyes, and his sight was restored. He got up and was baptized. When the scales came off, he saw and embraced the truth.

Thank You that You have given me the tongue of disciples [as One who is taught], That I may know how to sustain the weary with a word. He awakens Me morning by morning; He awakens My ear to listen as a disciple [as One who is taught]. Thank You, Lord, for the infilling of Your Word and my divine exchange. (Isaiah 50:4) Amen.

I will praise You; for I am fearfully and wonderfully made marvelous are Your works; and that my soul knows right well. I decree and receive the divine exchange and charge this Word to my soul. (Psalm 139:14)

I believe Your Word about me because You don't lie. My life belongs to You, Lord, and not to me. Thank You that You have given me so many options when I am depressed or feeling down. I draw my strength from You, Lord, and I will not depend on others to find my worth. I know You will help me to love myself.

I receive the Word that Jesus did not come to earth and give His life so that I would live a defeated life. He came so I would have the victory over death. I receive John 10:10: The thief comes only to steal and kill and destroy. I came that they may have and enjoy life, and have it in abundance.

Thank You that You will help me to desire life and to live fully in You. Thank You for Your Love for me. Amen.

8. Strongman of Jealousy

Jealousy: a feeling of unhappiness and anger caused by a belief that a loved one might be unfaithful; a feeling of unhappiness caused by wanting what someone else has; envy.

Characteristics and mannerisms: The definition contains its characteristics.

But if you have bitter jealousy and selfish ambition in your hearts, do not boast and be false to the truth. This is not the wisdom that comes down from above but is earthly, unspiritual, demonic. James 3:14-15

Prayer for deliverance

Dear Heavenly Father, I repent and ask forgiveness for allowing this strongman of jealousy to rule in any way in my life. I renounce it completely. I bind it and cast it out of me in the name of Jesus. I command you to leave now and get into the basket.

I hate the feelings of jealousy and I will not entertain them again. I know that You have created me with my own unique set of gifts and anointings and I am the only person on this earth that can accomplish what You have called me to do. I can't do what someone else has been empowered by You to do and they can't take anything from me that You have given me! Thank You for forgiving me. I command all envy and selfish ambition to leave me now and climb into the basket. (Next, you can give a good cough or blow out forcefully to get rid of any residue left from any of them.)

Thank You, Jesus, for delivering me of the spirits of jealousy, envy, and selfish ambition.

Holy Spirit, as I wait on You, please reveal if there are any other spirits that need to go that I have missed that operate with this spirit of jealously, envy, and spirit of selfish ambition. (Wait a moment to listen for the Holy Spirit to reveal any other demons that need to go. Next, raise the basket containing these evil spirits up to the Lord and wait a minute to see if you can see Him put anything in the basket as a divine exchange for you. If you don't see or hear anything, lower the basket back down and receive your divine exchange through your decree of infilling.)

Decree for infilling and divine exchange

I decree Ephesians 5:2-5: I will walk in love, as Christ loved me and gave Himself up for me, a fragrant offering and sacrifice to God. I fill my thoughts with praise and love for You and Your Word which washes me clean from all jealously, envy, and selfish ambition. I thank You for the divine exchange of peace and kindness towards others and genuine compassion.

I receive Your comforting love and acceptance of me as I am. No longer will I feel compelled to be like anyone else, or desire in an unhealthy way the things they have. I am content in You, Jesus. I receive 1 Corinthians 13:4-7 personally: Love is patient, love is kind. It does not envy, it does not boast, it is not proud. It does not dishonor others, it is not self-seeking, it is not easily angered, it keeps no record of wrongs. Love does not delight in evil but rejoices with the truth. It always protects, always trusts, always hopes, and always perseveres. Amen.

9. Strongman of Perversion

Perversion. Sexual perversion: a perverted form especially an aberrant sexual practice or interest, especially when habitual. The action of perverting: the condition of being perverted.

I'm not interested in a theological/political argument concerning the sexual sins that God calls perversions. I am quoting what He has to say in His word.

One day, each person will stand before the Lord to give an account of themselves while they lived on the earth. The Word says God hates this behavior. We pray for grace and mercy for anyone who has become a captive to this type of lifestyle.

Sexual Perversions: Homosexuality and Lesbianism

Abomination: something regarded with disgust or hatred: something abominable, extreme disgust and hatred, loathing.

You must not lie with a man as with a woman; that is an abomination. Leviticus 18:22

Because of this, God gave them over to shameful lusts. Even their women exchanged natural sexual relations for unnatural ones. In the same way the men also abandoned natural relations with women and were inflamed with lust for one another. Men committed shameful acts with other men and received in themselves the due penalty for their error. Romans 1:26-27 NIV

God makes it very clear in His Word how He feels about these perversions. He says if a man lays with a man, he will pay with diseases. Those who don't agree with what the Bible says and are Christians, have made a decision to believe a lie, or the demons are too strong to fight.

Now the Holy Spirit tells us clearly that in the last times some will turn away from the true faith; they will follow deceptive spirits and teachings that come from demons. 1 Timothy 4:1 NLT

I'm not saying that those that are caught in this perversion are not saved. Jesus loves the person but hates the sin. Our job isn't to judge; that's God's job. Our job is to pray. There is always hope if the person wants to be set free. Once they recognize this is a spiritual battle and there is a way out, they may take the way out of it. I pray for those who have been caught in this trap that the Lord will make an intervention of some kind on their behalf, and they will come to their senses.

For those who have children who were raised in the Lord and made these life choices, keep praying and be encouraged by 1 John 1:9.

If we confess our sins, he is faithful and just and will forgive us our sins and purify us from all unrighteousness. (NIV)

This gives us hope, because if they have ever accepted Jesus, God is able to fulfill His Word. Until the last breath leaves the body there is hope. God is willing to forgive.

For the unbelieving husband is sanctified through his wife, and the unbelieving wife is sanctified through her believing husband; for otherwise your children are unclean, but now they are holy. 1 Corinthians 7:14

As a word of encouragement, when a person choses to wave a rainbow banner for their purposes, they are not aware it is actually a prophetic statement. The rainbow is God's covenant symbol, and they are decreeing that they are going to come back under God's covenant as a child of God.

Characteristics and manifestations: This scripture defines this perversion.

Don't you realize that those who do wrong will not inherit the Kingdom of God? Don't fool yourselves. Those who indulge in sexual sin, or who worship idols, or commit adultery, or are male prostitutes, or practice homosexuality, or are thieves, or greedy people, or drunkards, or are abusive or cheat people none of these will inherit the Kingdom of God. Some of you were once like that. But you were cleansed; you were made holy; you were made right with God by calling on the name of the Lord Jesus Christ and by the Spirit of our God. 1 Corinthians 6:9-11 NLT

God is waiting to set a person free who is in bondage to any of these spirits.

Prayer for Deliverance

(Cast out each demon individually. Give a cough after each one.)

Lord, I ask You to forgive me for all my perverse sinful thoughts, words, and acts. I bind you strongman of perversion in every form that you manifest within me and command you to get out of me! You no longer have a home. I reject you completely. Every demon of sexual perversion assigned to my life, be bound, in the name of Jesus. Let any inherited demon of sexual perversion be permanently loosed away from me. I command any perverted demonic stronghold in my life to crumble and disappear. I cut myself off from every evil stranglehold of perversion that would try to hold onto me.

I loose myself from any soul ties that might be operating in my life connected to this sin, and I send back anything I have from anyone in the spiritual realm connected to it, and I demand they release anything of mine back to me. I command all perverse sexual desires to get out of me now and climb into the basket! You don't have a choice. Go now. I command the spirit of Homosexuality/Lesbianism to leave me now. Get into the basket. I command the spirit of sodomy to leave me now. Get into the basket. I command the spirit of pornography to leave me now. Get into the basket. I command any other foul or unclean spirits that are left within me to get out. Climb into the basket. I cut myself off and completely reject any perverted habits that have been inherited from my generational bloodline.

I repent and ask forgiveness for any lustful thoughts or acts. I renounce every claim I have given satan to my life, or sexuality through my sexual sins. I renounce every one of them and command the spirit of lust to get out of me now in Jesus' name. Climb into the basket. You no longer have any right to operate in me because I have repented and asked forgiveness. Every spiritual claim has been broken and deleted by the cross and blood of Jesus Christ. Get out of me now and climb into the basket.

I command any spirits of fornication and sexual immorality to get out of me and into the basket. Thank You, Lord, that all generational curses have been broken off me and any spirit of adultery that came from that source is leaving me. Get into the basket in Jesus' name.

I command my mind, body, and soul to be delivered of all lustful desires. I cast down every wicked unclean thought. I will not entertain it or yield to it in any way. I will not allow my eyes to sin by watching filthy things on TV or nasty movies again. They are a trap, and I slam that door and nail it shut.

(Next, you can give a good cough or blow out forcefully to get rid of any residue left by them.)

Thank You, Jesus, for delivering me of the spirit of perversion and every demon under that strongman including lust, fornication, and sexual immorality. (Raise the basket with the demons in it up to the Lord.)

Holy Spirit, as I wait on You, please reveal if there are any other spirits that I have missed that operate with this spirit of perversion that need to go. (After a short wait, raise the basket to the Lord. After another short wait, lower it back down and accept your divine exchange and infilling.)

Decree for infilling and the divine exchange

Thank You, Lord Jesus, for delivering my soul and my body completely from the spirit, and every demon who promotes and influences me towards sexual perversion. Thank You for setting me free from the demons that are included with the spirit of lust.

I decree Galatians 5:16. I say then, I shall walk in the Spirit, and I shall not fulfill the lust of the flesh. I receive my new spiritual mind and Your cleansing and restoration to my mind, soul, and body. I praise You for my victory. I decree I am spiritually minded and no longer carnally minded.

Holy Spirit, wash me clean as I surrender my mind, will, and emotions to You. Fill me with Your power. Guide and direct my path and send help from the sanctuary to enable me to stay clean before You. Help me to hate the sin.

Thank You, that today is my day of deliverance and that You have extended Your grace and mercy and forgiveness for my sins, and I receive it all for my victory. You have just delivered me from bondage into freedom. Father God, You have been faithful to hear my prayers and set me free and I am so grateful! Thank You!

I declare Psalm 85:8 over myself: I will hear [with expectant hope] what God the Lord will say, For He will speak peace to His people, to His godly ones.

Thank You for my divine exchange. I will study Your Word and it will wash my soul clean. Your Word has the power within itself, to fulfill itself within me, and I receive the truth of all that it has to say to me which will transform me completely into who I am meant to be.

I receive Your perfect peace. I decree Philippians 4:13. I can do all things through Christ who strengthens me. I dedicate my body and my sexuality to Jesus Christ. Amen.

10. Strongman of haughtiness

Haughtiness: scornful, prideful, snobbishness, arrogance.

Characteristics and manifestations: Pride and arrogance.

Pride goes before destruction, And a haughty spirit before a fall. It is better to be humble in spirit with the lowly than to divide the spoil with the proud (haughty, arrogant). Proverbs 16:18-19

When pride comes, then comes disgrace, but with the humble is wisdom. Proverbs 11:2

Prayer for deliverance

I repent and ask forgiveness for having a haughty and prideful spirit. I thank You, Jesus, and receive Your forgiveness for this sin. I bind the strongman spirit of haughtiness and pride and command them to get out of me. Leave me now! You no longer have anything to hang onto. Get out of me and get into the basket right now.

Thank You, Jesus, for delivering me of the spirit of haughtiness and pride. (Next, you give a good cough or blow out forcefully to get rid of any residue from it.)

Holy Spirit, as I wait on You, please reveal if there are any other spirits that I have missed that need to go that operate with this spirit of haughtiness and pride. (Next, lift the basket up to the Lord and wait a minute to see if He places anything in the basket for you. Then you can lower the basket back down.)

Prayer for infilling

Thank You, Jesus, for delivering me. I decree that I am replacing haughtiness and pride with Godly humility. The Word says in James 4:10, that when I humble myself in the sight of the Lord, He shall lift me up.

Lord, I know that You love a humble spirit. You say in Isaiah 66:2, All these things my hand has made, and so all these things came to be, declares the Lord. But this is the one to whom I will look: he who is humble and contrite in spirit and trembles at my word. Thank you, Lord, for helping me to develop a humble and contrite spirit. Amen

11. Strongman of rebellion

Rebellion: an act of violence or open resistance to an established government or ruler.

Characteristics and manifestations: Rebellion is opposition to authority. Rebellion against God's authority was humanity's first sin. Man likes to think he is his own boss. That rebellion found in the man's heart is the root of all sin. Rebellion leads to division and strife.

Prayer for deliverance

Dear Heavenly Father, I come to You now in Jesus' name. I repent and ask forgiveness for the sin of rebellion in my life. I repent of all rebellion, disobedience, stubbornness, and obstinance which is bullheadedness. I bind you, strongman of rebellion, and cast you out of me. Get out, in Jesus' name! Get into the basket. (Give a cough after each demon you cast out.)

I command disobedience to get out of me now and climb into the basket. I command the spirit of stubbornness to get out of me and climb into the basket. I command the spirit of obstinance or bullheadedness to get out of me now and climb into the basket. Thank You, Jesus, for forgiving me of these sins and setting me free of the demons attached to the sins. (Next, you can give a good cough or blow out forcefully to get rid of any residue left of them.)

Holy Spirit, as I wait on You. Please reveal if there are any other spirits that I have missed that operate with this spirit of rebellion. (Raise the basket up to the Lord for Your divine exchange. Wait a minute to see if the Holy Spirit says or does

142

something. Then lower the basket back down and make Your decree of infilling.)

Decree of infilling and divine exchange

I reject all rebellion in my life. I receive my divine exchange by decreeing Colossians 3:12-14. I will put on then, as God's chosen one, holy and beloved, a compassionate heart, kindness, humility, meekness, and patience, bearing with others and, if one has a complaint against another, we will forgive each other; as the Lord has forgiven me, I must forgive. And above all these, I put on love, which binds everything together in perfect harmony. (ESV) Amen.

I decree over myself that I am now delivered and set free from any stiff neck because I have cast out all stubbornness.

12. Strongman of Antichrist

Antichrist : The antichrist is the opposite of Christ. Just as Christ came to earth to do God's will, the job of the antichrist is to do the will of satan. He opposes God and His ways. His whole ambition is to be like God in power and might, and he works for this with all his might, night, and day.

When describing the antichrist, the scriptures say:

> *Who opposes and exalts himself above all that is called God, or that is worshipped, so that he sits as God in the temple of God, showing himself that he is God.*
> *2 Thessalonians 2:4 NKJV*

> *For many deceivers have gone out into the world who do not confess Jesus Christ as coming in the flesh. This is a deceiver and an antichrist. 2 John 1:7 NKJV*

A Christian may think they don't have to deal with this strongman, but if they have been involved in witchcraft of any kind, this could be a real issue. It may be as serious as satanic rituals, or it may be seeking out a fortune teller as a joke, or in fun, without understanding that repercussions could show up against them years later. Some have used Ouija Boards or tarot cards as kids, not understanding the consequences. There are a lot of streaming games out there that have a person make an oath to an entity. Targeted at kids especially, they don't understand the seriousness of how that can affect their lives. Anything we look to in the supernatural that doesn't look to God is idolatrous to Him and can be viewed as a type of antichrist.

> ...and no wonder, since Satan himself masquerades as an angel of light. So it is no great surprise if his servants also masquerade as servants of righteousness, but their end will correspond with their deeds.
> 2 Corinthians 11:14-15

Characteristics and manifestations: This spirit causes a person to oppose the things and words of Christ. A Christian can have this spirit and not know it, especially if they have been involved in the occult or witchcraft before being converted to Christianity and haven't gone through deliverance and evicted this strongman and his servants.

The spirit of God within them wants to pursue the things of the Kingdom of God, but the persons old unrenewed carnal man's soul nature, where this spirit lives, will fight against everything godly they are trying to pursue. It constantly works at getting the person to embrace unbelief and entices the person in the wrong direction.

If you find yourself thinking that you want proof that the scriptures are true, then you might be battling this spirit within. This spirit hates the prophets and the prophetic and will always try to hinder and obstruct what God wants to share through prophetic people.

Prayer for deliverance

Dear Jesus, I believe that You are the Son of God, and You are the only way to salvation. I repent and ask forgiveness and renounce my sins. Thank You, Jesus, that You died on the cross to redeem me from my sins. I accept Your perfect sacrifice for my sin. I am washed and cleansed by Your blood and no longer guilty.

In Jesus' name, I bind and command the strongman spirit of antichrist to leave me now. Get out! I demand that you get in the basket and do it now. You don't have a choice because I speak to you with the authority of Jesus Christ. (Now you can give a good cough or blow out forcefully to get rid of it. Try to see it getting out of you and into the basket. If you can't see it, it's ok. Believe in faith that it has left you and gotten into the basket.) *Thank You, Father, for delivering me of the spirit of antichrist.*

a. Demon spirit of error

We are of God. He who knows God hears us; he who is not of God does not hear us. By this we know the spirit of truth and the spirit of error. 1 John 4:6 NKJV.

Characteristics and manifestations: Error comes from both the carnal mind and the demon spirit. The spirit of error and mistake leads to inaccurate judgment. People make decisions that lead to wrong actions. Their wrong actions eventually lead to failure in life. Many have lost their jobs, positions, families, and many other things because of actions they mistakenly believed to be right but were wrong because they listened to a spirit of error. It is the spirit of error that will make a Christian indulge in fornication or adultery or some other sin continuously, and still believe he or she is on the right path to heaven.

145

Prayer for deliverance

Dear Jesus, I repent, renounce, and ask forgiveness for harboring a spirit of error. I can see that it causes me to constantly make mistakes in my life which cause problems for me then I begin to doubt that You love me. I bind and command the spirit of error to go in the name of Jesus. I cast you out of me. Now leave. Get out of me and into the basket now. You no longer have a home in me. (Give a good cough or blow out forcefully to get rid of it.)

b. Demon spirit of whoredoms

Whoredom: the practice of whoring: prostitution. 2: faithless, unworthy, or idolatrous practices or pursuits.

> *My people consult a wooden idol, and a diviner's rod speaks to them. A spirit of prostitution leads them astray; they are unfaithful to their God. Hosea 4:12 NIV*

Other translations say *whoredoms* instead of prostitution.

Characteristics and manifestations: Idolatry is a manifestation or symptom of this spirit of whoredoms. If a person collects items, lots of the same items, they can become idols to them at least in God's eyes. Some people worship sports figures, cars, singers, clothes, and any number of things. Money—either too little or too much can be an idol.

It's important that each person examines themselves. This spirit of whoredom causes people to seek out alternate ways into the supernatural realm instead of seeking Christ and entering the supernatural realm through the Holy Spirit.

> *Their doings will not permit them to return to their God, for the spirit of harlotry is within them and they know not the Lord [they do not recognize, appreciate, give heed to, or cherish the Lord]. Hosea 5:4 AMPC*

146

Prayer for deliverance

Dear Jesus, I repent, renounce, and ask forgiveness for harboring a spirit of whoredoms. My goal is to chase after the things of Jesus Christ and no other god. In the name of Jesus, I command you evil spirit to get out of me and into the basket now. You no longer have a home in me. Leave. Holy Spirit, reveal to me the things in my life that I have made into an idol so I can get rid of any idolatry I might be guilty of. (Give a good cough or blow out forcefully to get rid of it.)

c. Demon spirit of divination

Divination: The practice of determining the hidden significance or cause of events, sometimes foretelling the future, by various psychological and other occultic techniques.

> *Do not turn to mediums [who pretend to consult the dead] or to spiritists [who have spirits of divination]; do not seek them out to be defiled by them. I am the Lord your God. Leviticus 19:31*

Characteristics and manifestations: Prophesying the future through various occultic means. Tarot cards, fortune tellers, mediums, tea leaves, astrology, reading palms.

Prayer for deliverance

I repent, renounce, and ask forgiveness for any occult participation, in Jesus' name. I close every doorway of demonic invasion into my life, in the name of Jesus. I cancel every demonic agenda to deceive me and get me off track from my destiny, in Jesus' name.

In the name of Jesus, I command you to get out of me and into the basket now. You no longer have a home in me. Leave. (Give a good cough or blow out forcefully to get rid of it.)

d. Demon of spirit of familiar spirits

Familiar spirit: a spirit or demon that serves or prompts an individual. the spirit of a dead person invoked by a medium to advise or prophesy.

> *A man also or woman that hath a familiar spirit, or that is a wizard, shall surely be put to death: they shall stone them with stones: their blood shall be upon them.*
> *Leviticus 20:27 KJV*

This is Old Testament law that demanded that a medium or a witch would physically be put to death, which isn't the case today. But it is clear how the Lord feels about this spirit.

Characteristics and manifestations: A familiar spirit is sometimes called a 'spirit guide' in the kingdom of darkness. Deception is always present in one's relationship with a familiar spirit. It is the counterfeit of the Holy Spirit. Usually, those that have a familiar spirit believe that their spirit companion is good, rather than evil and that something beneficial will come out of that relationship. They may believe that the spirit is a true supporter who will provide them with helpful information.

A person may even believe that the familiar spirit is the Holy Spirit. The person with a familiar spirit may not recognize that it is a spirit entity not from God with whom he is having a relationship. They may believe they have contacted God's spiritual realm. They may be ensnared, not because they are seeking something evil, but because they are seeking something good in the wrong way.

The person thinks the voice they are hearing is God's, or a loved one that they are seeking to connect with. When the things that they are told about their future never come to pass, because demons don't know the future only the past, it will cause them to eventually begin to doubt God and move into unbelief.

A familiar spirit can be assigned to people or their family bloodline. This spirit works through mediums and operates as a counterfeit holy spirit.

> *So, Saul died for his breach of faith. He broke faith with the Lord in that he did not keep the command of the Lord, and consulted a medium, seeking guidance.*
> *1 Chronicles 10:13*

When people are curious or desperate to connect with a loved one who has passed away or is missing and they go to a fortune-teller, also known a medium, they open the door for a familiar spirit to enter. I have heard many people say that the spirit of a loved one who has passed away comes at times and comforts them. This is a demon and not the spirit of the departed loved one.

> *And just as it is appointed and destined for all men to die once and after this [comes certain] judgment.*
> *Hebrews 9:27 ESV*

This means that a person isn't going to die and then come back in some other form. A familiar spirit can disguise itself to smell like the departed person: perfume smell or aftershave, pipe smoke. They will use any means possible to fool the person. The same with those in the occult that do handwriting. They become the medium through which the familiar spirit works, and their handwriting will be an exact copy of the departed loved one.

Because the demon is very familiar with a person's past, they can provide many details to prove that they are the person who has died, but they aren't.

God Himself will comfort a person who has lost a loved one. These experiences are different from dreams and visions that the Lord may give a person of their loved one. That's why the Scripture says to test the spirits. There are many that are not godly.

I don't intend to offend anyone. I'm not saying that God doesn't send His symbols of comfort, such as a particular bird or butterfly, symbols that the deceased liked. That particular symbol is not the person or their spirit. Even though they may have said, "If you see a redbird, that's me." That person and their spirit, if they were saved, is in heaven. But the symbol is not the person coming back to comfort them. The Holy Spirit is the one comforting them with the memory, so give the glory to God and recognize that He has sent a symbol of comfort and encouragement.

Prayer for deliverance

I repent, renounce, and ask forgiveness for harboring a familiar spirit. I loose my destiny from every grip of occult demons, in the name of Jesus. In the name of Jesus, I command you to get out of me and into the basket now. You no longer have a home in me. Leave. (Give a good cough or blow out forcefully to get rid of it.)

e. Demon spirit of sorcery

Sorcery: the use of power gained from the assistance or control of evil spirits especially for divining. A person who uses witchcraft or sorcery, especially to reanimate dead people or to foretell the future by communicating with them.

Characteristics and manifestations:

Now the works of the flesh are evident, which are: adultery, fornication, uncleanness, lewdness, idolatry, sorcery, hatred, contentions, jealousies, outbursts of

wrath, selfish ambitions, dissensions, heresies.
Galatians 5:19-20 NKJV

Prayer for deliverance

I repent, renounce, and ask forgiveness for harboring a spirit of sorcery and every other demon with it, such as adultery, fornication, uncleanness, lewdness, idolatry, hatred, contentions, jealousies, outbursts of wrath, selfish ambitions, dissensions, heresies. In the name of Jesus, I command you all to get out of me and into the basket now. You no longer have a home in me. Leave. (Give a good cough or blow out forcefully to get rid of it.)

Holy Spirit, as I wait on You, shine Your light from the bottom of my feet up through my body to the top of my head, driving out anything that is not of You. Reveal to me if there are any other spirits that need to leave me that operate with this sorcery spirit.

f. Demon spirit of witchcraft

Ye shall not ... use enchantment, nor observe times.
Leviticus 19:26 KJV

Characteristics and manifestations: Fortunetelling-soothsayer, satanist-witch or wiccan-warlock-druid-pagan, astrology, horoscopes, Ouija board, tarot cards, palm reading, reading tea leaves. Casting spells and sending curses.

Prayer for deliverance

I repent, renounce, and ask forgiveness for harboring and being involved with any form of the spirit of witchcraft. In the name of Jesus, I command you to get out of me and into the basket now. You no longer have a home. You must go now! (Give a good cough or blow out forcefully to get rid of it.)

151

g. Demon of a lying spirit

Lying: a person who tells lies. Opposite of the truth, deception, dishonesty, deceit, corruption, cheating.

Characteristics and manifestations: The Bible says that satan is the great liar. This spirit convinces the person to believe lies and will also compel people to tell lies. Then they convince them to believe their lies so when they share them with others, they convince them to believe the lies too.

The devil places veils over the eyes of the understanding of a person. He convinces them that they are walking in the truth, but they aren't. The apostle Paul is the best example of this. He was a great religious leader, but he had a veil of religious deception over the eyes of his understanding so he would reject the truth. God sovereignly removed the veils/scales from his eyes so he could see and embrace the truth.

> *...and immediately there fell from his eyes as it had been scales: and he received sight forthwith, and arose, and was baptized. Acts 9:18 KJV*

The Lord allowed a lying spirit to enter the false prophets.

> *And there came forth a spirit, and stood before the Lord, and said, I will persuade him. And the Lord said unto him, wherewith? And he said, I will go forth, and I will be a lying spirit in the mouth of all his prophets. And he said, Thou shalt persuade him, and prevail also: go forth and do so. Now therefore, behold, the Lord hath put a lying spirit in the mouth of all these thy prophets, and the Lord hath spoken evil concerning thee. 1 Kings 22:21-23 KJV*

> *You belong to your father, the devil, and you want to carry out your father's desires. He was a murderer from the beginning, not holding to the truth, for there is no*

*truth in him. When he lies, he speaks his native
language, for he is a liar and the father of lies.
John 8:44 NIV*

Prayer for deliverance

*I repent, renounce, and ask forgiveness for harboring a lying
spirit. In the name of Jesus, I command you to get out of me
and into the basket now. You no longer have a home in me.
Leave. Climb into the basket right now in Jesus' name!* (Give a
good cough or blow out forcefully to get rid of it.)

As we conclude our deliverance, stay alert in your life for any
strongmen or demons we didn't kick out. If by chance you
should discover any, you can use these prayers and decrees
to get rid of them just as you did the rest.

**Decree of infilling for the divine exchange from the
deliverance of the strongman of anti-christ and
demons of error, whoredoms, divination, familiar
spirit, sorcery, witchcraft, lying spirit, and rebellion
who were all under the authority of the antichrist
spirit.**

*Thank You Jesus for forgiving me for my sin of placing myself
in a position to receive these antichrist witchcraft spirits. I
have renounced and asked forgiveness for each one and I
have been completely delivered from the spirit of the
antichrist and the demons under him. I decree and believe
that Jesus Christ is the son of God and that He died on the
cross to pay for my sins.*

*I decree that any sufferings that came because of past errors
and mistakes will be removed from my life and family, in
Jesus' name. I decree the spirit of wisdom and understanding
will come upon me for the accurate evaluation of things that
have to do with decisions that I make, in Jesus' name. I thank*

you Jesus that you will give me a gift of Godly discernment, so I am able to make good choices.

I am completely dedicated to You. Thank You for filling me with the truth. I thank You that I am wonderfully made to show forth Your glory in my life.

I believe the truth. Jesus died and was resurrected from the grave and is alive today. I accept His perfect sacrifice for my sins, I am washed and cleansed by the blood of Jesus for my sins. I have been delivered and set free, in the name of Jesus.

I fill the vacant space place that the strongman and the demons under him left with Your word. I receive the divine exchange of truth for lies. The spirit of truth has liberated me. You tell me in John 8:32, "And I shall know the truth, and the truth shall make me free."

John 16:13: "But when He, the Spirit of truth, comes, He will guide me into all the truth; for He will not speak on His own initiative, but whatever He hears, He will speak; and He will disclose to me what is to come."

John 14:17: Jesus is the Spirit of truth. The world cannot accept Him because it neither sees Him nor knows Him. But I know Him, for He lives with me and will be in me.

I decree I am completely pro-Christ. I will depend on the word of God and the Holy Spirit to guide me into all truth and to help me to recognize sin for what it is. I will never operate under the bondage of any of these spirits again.

I will have a hunger for Your word and as I read it I will be washed clean. Expose my enemies of the unseen realm that attempt to imitate the Holy Spirit, in Jesus' name, Amen.

Chapter 12

Keeping Your deliverance

What does the Bible tell us about contending?

To *contend* is to fight for your victory. God has given us the victory. We have gotten rid of the demons who, in some cases, were the root cause of our compulsive negative behavior. But we must now fight against the familiar habits that we have developed and become familiar with over years. These habits have worked against us but made the demons happy.

The Lord is with us, and our victory is totally in Him. A person must not begin to think "I have this" and let their guard down. To keep our deliverance, we must stay in the Word and communion with God daily. When we do this, the old unrenewed man in us will pass away, and it won't even be a struggle. Before long, the things that tempted us before won't be a temptation any longer. I can say this from practical experience.

When we fill our minds with thoughts about Jesus and His Word, we think less and less about addictions or issues that we have struggled with in the past. But we can't let our guard down because the enemy is watching for an open door into us so he can come back.

It may be necessary for some to set up counseling to help them get through their difficult times, and that is wisdom to do so. It's not a weakness. It's recognizing that you need help to stay free and getting that help.

It is not God's fault if a person backslides into their old ways. God is faithful to deliver, but man doesn't always stay faithful to keep his deliverance.

Contending prayer decree to keep our deliverance:

Dear Heavenly Father, Thank You for setting me totally free. You say in 2 Corinthians 3:17, Now the Lord is the Spirit, and where the Spirit of the Lord is, there is freedom. (NIV)

I decree Your Words over myself: The Spirit of the LORD shall rest upon me, the Spirit of wisdom and understanding, the Spirit of counsel and might, the Spirit of knowledge and of the fear of the LORD, and I will delight in the fear of the Lord. (Isaiah 11:2–3 NIV)

I decree, once again, the divine exchange that You gave me. You will fill every empty place within me with the fruits of Your spirit. The fruit of Your Spirit is love, joy, peace, forbearance, kindness, goodness, faithfulness, gentleness, and self-control. Against such things, there is no law. (Galatians 5:22-23 NIV)

I determine daily to put on the whole armor of God, as it says in Ephesians, "Finally, be strong in the Lord and in the strength of his might. Put on the whole armor of God that you may be able to stand against the schemes of the devil. For we do not wrestle against flesh and blood, but against the rulers, against the authorities, against the cosmic powers over this present darkness, against the spiritual forces of evil in the heavenly places." (Ephesians 6:10-12 ESV)

I will continue to submit myself therefore to God. I will resist the devil, and he will flee from me. I will draw near to God, and he will draw near to me. (James 4:7 ESV)

I do not have to be afraid of failure, as I take positive steps to ensure my continued victory. I will be intentional. I will develop good habits to replace bad ones. Thank You that You will help me. Your Word is a shield of protection around me.

The Lord is my strength and my shield; My heart trusts in Him, and I am helped; Therefore, my heart exults, and with my song I shall thank Him. (Psalm 28:7 ESV)

He has delivered me from the power of darkness and translated me into the kingdom of the Son of His love, in whom I have redemption through His blood, the forgiveness of sins." (Colossians 1:13 NIV)

As I have been delivered and healed, I am willing to be used powerfully by You. I am eager to extend my hand to the poor and needy and not hide from the needs of my family, my flesh, and blood. I decree Your Word which says,

"Then my light will break out like the dawn, and my healing will quickly spring forth; Your righteousness will go before me. The glory of the Lord will be my rear guard. "Then I will call, and the Lord will answer; I will cry for help, and He will say, 'Here I am.' (Isaiah 58:8)

As I have repented for judging others and any other sinful negative thing, I have been guilty of that which includes all the negative words spoken out of my mouth. I decree what You say over me.

Then my light will rise in the darkness and my gloom will become like midday. And the Lord will continually guide me, and satisfy my soul in scorched and dry places, and give strength to my bones, and I will be like a watered garden and like a spring of water whose waters do not fail. And I will rebuild the ancient ruins; I will raise up and restore the age-old foundations [of buildings that have been laid waste]; I will be called Repairer of the Breach, Restorer of Streets with Dwellings. (Isaiah 58:6-12) Amen.

About the Author

Jeanette is in active ministry. In 1997, she and her husband, Bud, founded and are the co-owners of Glorious Creations. Glorious Creations is a Worship and Praise adornment company. Jeanette is ordained as a minister through Gospel Crusade and has been in full time ministry since 1998. Jeanette and her husband are active members of New Heart Ministries in Coldwater, Michigan. She is a member of Aglow International and an intercessor for Southwest Michigan under the leadership of Barbara Yoder of Breakthrough Apostolic Ministries (BAM), and a member intercessor for Heartland Apostolic Prayer Network (HAPN) for Michigan under Anita Christopher.

Cover art by James Nesbit

Overseer of Prepare the Way Ministries International, James has been used by God to help prepare the way for the coming awakening in America through strategic level intercessory assignments. Overseer of Mountain Alliance of Illinois, HAPN and RPN state coordinator for Illinois, and overseer for the region named Joy Number Nine, which includes the states of Missouri, Kentucky, Illinois, Indiana, Ohio, and Michigan.

The Lord has seen fit to allow his artwork to be displayed in many nations throughout the earth. Visit the online gallery at www.jamesnart.com. He can also be reached through www.ptwministries.com or nesb7@aol.com

Other resources from Jeanette Strauss

Heavenly Impact
Symbolic Praise, Worship, and Intercession
Earth As It Is In Heaven"

This book is a must read for those seeking a Biblical foundation for the use of symbolic tools of praise, worship, and intercession. This information presents clear guidelines concerning their proper place and use.

Heavenly Impact guides you through Bible history and explains the relevance of worship adornment as it identifies strategic value to worship. Scripture references reveal that our actions on earth truly do have a "Heavenly Impact". Tools covered: flags, billows, Mat-teh', shofar, streamers, tabrets, and veils, vocabulary of movement and Biblical color symbolism. Also available in Spanish. $14.00

Heavenly Impact - Teaching Bundle

We have had such a wonderful response to the *Heavenly Impact* book, a *Teachers Manual* and *Student Workbook* are now available for use in teaching Dance Ministry or small Life Groups. The *Teachers Manual* includes Prophetic Activations and Exercises at the end of the chapters and different discussion topics. Each chapter includes the questions, along with the answers, for the teacher's convenience and references the page the answer is on in the *Heavenly Impact* book. The *Student Workbook* includes the questions, prophetic activations and exercises, and a section of biblical significance of colors. We also include a "Certificate Of Completion" suitable for framing. Set includes one *Heavenly Impact*, one *Teachers Manual*, one *Student Manual*, and one Certificate of Completion. $40.00

Redeem Your Home

This book contains Biblical teaching about the necessity of spiritually cleansing your home, apartment, or business. It includes step-by-step instructions with prayers to read that will insure the dedication of your home, apartment, or business to the Lord. This insures the removal of any demonic presence that may be residing within it. Don't wait; set your home, apartment, business, and family free today! $10.00

Redeem Your Home & Anointing Oil

This set includes one copy of Redeem Your Home, and a vial of oil. The oil is a combination of olive oil from Israel and a kosher wine, which serves as a symbol of the Blood of Christ as the sacrificial lamb. This oil/wine combination is to be placed over the doorposts and lintels as a symbol of covenant, for all of the heavenly realm to see. This wine is appropriately named "Shalom," which makes a prophetic statement that your home and every room you anoint are under God's covenant protection.

The word *shalom* means "peace," which includes being safe in mind, body, or estate. It speaks of a sense of completeness and inner tranquility; nothing missing, nothing broken. The common western definition of peace is the absence of conflict or war and fits well with what we are using it for as we anoint our homes. In Israel today, when you greet someone or say goodbye, you say, 'Shalom.' You are literally saying, "May you be full of well-being" or, "May health and prosperity be upon you." A $20 value for $18.00.

From God's Hands To Your Land

The Bible establishes the spiritual relationship between God and His land. The Lord desires to pour out His blessings on your land, but Scripture says that His blessings can be blocked.

The Lord, as the Owner of the original title deed of all real estate, gave us the responsibility to subdue and take dominion over the land. Included in this book are step-by-step instructions for the Restoration Ceremony, with prayers and decrees to recite as you reconcile and redeem your land that will ensure that His blessings will flow freely on your land with no hindrances. Also available in Spanish. $10.00

Bless Your Land Kit

This kit contains the items you will need for the Restoration Ceremony: 1 copy of the book, *From God's Hands to Your Land,* 4 communion cups with wafers, milk, honey, harvest seeds, consecration oil, a Title Deed. $20.00

Heavenly Advance
Prophetic Intercession
Activating the Forces of God's Angelic Armies

This book describes what the term "prophetic intercession" means, and how it has played a significant role throughout history in changing the lives, communities, and the course of nations. You will read examples of actions of prophetic intercession as performed by Jesus, His disciples, and others. These symbolic actions, directed by God, mobilized the forces of angelic hosts to move on their behalf to see His purposes fulfilled on the earth.

If you haven't yet spoken or performed an action of prophetic intercession, this book will lead the way for you to enter and experience the Kingdom of God on the earth in a new way.

From the Courtroom of Heaven to the Throne Room of Grace and Mercy

As a born-again Christian, I had never given the Courtroom of Heaven a thought. Then, in an answer to prayer for our daughter who was backslidden, the Lord gave me a dream that contained a strategy to use in heaven's Courtroom. As a result, she was set free and restored. Included is the strategy that can be used to win your specific petition in the Heavenly Court. This revised edition includes additional revelation from the Lord, and more testimonies to the goodness of God when we take our petitions to Him in His Courtroom. $14.00 Also available

From the Courtroom of Heaven to the Throne Room of Grace and Mercy *Prayers and Petitions*

This is a companion to the book *From the Courtroom of Heaven to the Throne Room of Grace and Mercy.* It contains examples of prayers and petitions you can use in the Courtroom. They are "Court ready" and can be read, word for word, by filling in the blank with the name of the people and situations you are praying for. These prayers are in addition to those included in *From the Courtroom of Heaven to the Throne Room of Grace and Mercy.* $13.00

From the Courtroom of Heaven to the Throne Room of Grace and Mercy Teaching Bundle

Everything you need to teach a small group study or class at church in one neat package. *The Bundle* includes one copy of the book *"From the Courtroom of Heaven to the Throne of Grace and Mercy"* and one of the companion *Prayer and Petition* book, along with a flash drive that includes a teaching outline to print, and a Power Point presentation. $50.00.

Additional Courtroom books can be purchased at a 20% discount when ordering this set. To get the discounted price, call to order, or email us at Jeanette@gloriouscreations.net.

OTHER PRODUCTS AVAILABLE

- All types of Worship Flags for Praise
- Angel Wings
- Anointing Oils and Balm of Gilead
- Books
- Books By: Jeanette Strauss
- CD's and DVD's
- Children's Praise
- Christian Prophetic Art
- Dance Garments for Praise and Worship Dance
- Debi Woods Calligraphy
- Fabrics, Tinsel, Appliqués & More
- Fan Streamers
- Gift Certificates
- Glory Rings / Glory Wavers
- Jewelry
- Prayer Shawls & Judaica
- Reduced Priced Items
- Shofars, Ram Horns & Trumpets
- Streamers
- Sword
- Tabrets/Glory Hoops
- Tambourine
- Threshing Floor Prayer Mats
- Veils/Mantles
- Wall Hangings/Banners

Glorious Creations
1114 Robinson Road, Quincy, Michigan 49082
(517) 639-4395 www.glariouscreations.net

ORDER FORM

Produce	*Price*	*Quantity*		*Total*
From God's Hand To Your Land	$10.00	x _____	=	_____
De las Manos de Dios a Tu Tierra	$10.00	x _____	=	_____
Bless Your Land Kit	$20.00	x _____	=	_____
Redeem Your Home	$10.00	x _____	=	_____
Redeem Your Home & Oil	$18.00	x _____	=	_____
From the Courtroom of Heaven	$14.00	x _____	=	_____
From the Courtroom of Heaven Prayers and Petitions	$13.00	x _____	=	_____
From the Courtroom of Heaven Teaching Bundle	$50.00	x _____	=	_____
Heavenly Impact	$14.00	x _____	=	_____
Impacto Divino	$14.00	x _____	=	_____
Heavenly Impact Teaching Bundle	$40.00	x _____	=	_____
Heavenly Impact Student Workbook	$13.00	x _____	=	_____
Deliverance	$12.00	x _____	=	_____

Total due for Product   _____

Shipping & Handling   _____

Total Amount Due   _____

Shipping & Handling:	
0-$9.95	$ 4.00
$10 - $19.95	$ 6.00
$20.00 - $39.95	$ 9.00
$40.00 -$60.00	$10.00
We ship books USPS	